A CREATOR'S GUIDE TO
TRANSMEDIA
STORYTELLING

A CREATOR'S GUIDE TO
TRANSMEDIA STORYTELLING

How to Captivate and Engage Audiences Across Multiple Platforms

ANDREA PHILLIPS

NEW YORK   CHICAGO   SAN FRANCISCO
LISBON   LONDON   MADRID   MEXICO CITY   MILAN
NEW DELHI   SAN JUAN   SEOUL   SINGAPORE
SYDNEY   TORONTO

2 3 4 5 6 7 8 9 0   QTN/QTN   1 8 7 6 5 4 3

ISBN 978-0-07-179152-6
MHID   0-07-179152-3

e-ISBN 978-0-07-179153-3
e-MHID   0-07-179153-1

Design by Lee Fukui and Mauna Eichner

McGraw-Hill books are available at special quantity discounts to use as premiums and sales promotions or for use in corporate training programs. To contact a representative, please e-mail us at bulksales@mcgraw-hill.com.

This book is printed on acid-free paper.

Library of Congress Cataloging-in-Publication Data

Phillips, Andrea.
  A creator's guide to transmedia storytelling : how to captivate and engage audiences across multiple platforms / by Andrea Phillips.
    p. cm.
  ISBN 978-0-07-179152-6 (alk. paper) — ISBN 0-07-179152-3 (alk. paper)
  1. Digital storytelling. 2. Interactive multimedia. 3. Internet entertainment industry. 4. Marketing—Psychological aspects. I. Title.
  QA76.76.I59P496 2012
  006.7—dc23
                                                                                              2012002246

For Dave Szulborski

Contents

SECTION I

SECTION II

STORYTELLING

SECTION III

STRUCTURE

PRODUCTION

THE BIG PICTURE

Preface

There's never been a more exciting time to be a storyteller.

Whether you're a filmmaker, a writer, a marketer, or any other kind of storyteller, it's easier than ever before to get your story in front of an audience. New platforms and business models are emerging, gatekeepers are falling, and the possibilities can take your breath away. Creators are learning how to spin these platforms together into complex, integrated works in which the whole is greater than the sum of its parts—that's transmedia.

Best practices and conventional wisdom are emerging, slowly but surely, as creators at the edge of innovation learn from their successes and failures. But little of this knowledge is making it past the tight constraints of NDAs and whispered conversations in convention hallways.

We need a public conversation sharing that knowledge.

By writing *A Creator's Guide to Transmedia Storytelling*, I'm doing my part to get that conversation started. I've shared what I've learned from my years in transmedia, working on high-profile, award-winning, and innovative projects like *The Maester's*

Path for HBO's *Game of Thrones*, *The 2012 Experience* for Sony Pictures, the indie commercial game *Perplex City*, the nonprofit human rights game *America 2049*, and many others.

This book will help you to get your bearings and prepare for your start as a transmedia creator (or improve your craft, if you're already in). We'll start out with a dose of transmedia history for perspective, cover some storytelling basics, and then move on to more rigorous elements of craft and production: how to write when your story is fragmented across multiple media; how to structure a story across platforms so that it still feels like one piece (and how not to); how to find the money, how to put together a team, and how to incorporate new media.

You'll also find interviews with groundbreaking creators known for such works as the blockbuster indie film *The Blair Witch Project*, MTV's immersive series *Valemont*, and phenomenal marketing campaigns like *The Dark Knight*'s award-winning *Why So Serious?* Every one of these men and women has been inspiring and influential to my own practice, and I hope they'll be enlightening to you, as well.

Good luck on your upcoming adventures—there's nothing as creatively fulfilling as making a well-executed transmedia narrative, and I am delighted to share that joy with you.

A CREATOR'S GUIDE TO
TRANSMEDIA
STORYTELLING

SECTION I

INTRODUCTION TO TRANSMEDIA

1 Once Upon a Time . . .

Anna Heath was the mother of three young children and a brilliant languages professor. She was also a fictional character—part of the game *Perplex City*, which was a two-year-long treasure hunt developed by UK games company Mind Candy that attracted tens of thousands of players and sold more than a million puzzle cards.

One night in late July 2006, Anna disappeared. Her colleagues desperately tried to put together the pieces of where she had last been seen and by whom. Her husband appealed to the public for something, anything, that would ensure her safe return home.

But it was all for nothing. The search for Anna eventually turned up her body in the catacombs beneath the city. She had been brutally tortured and murdered while investigating a series of thefts from the academy where she was employed.

Anna Heath of *Perplex City*
Image used with permission of Mind Candy

The audience was devastated by her loss. They reported feeling as if they'd been punched in the gut, that they hadn't seen it coming, that they were surprised at the depth of grief they felt for an imaginary person.

Heartfelt condolence emails to all the other characters in the game flooded in. Players even cast about for a real-world way to honor Anna's memory. Together, some audience members folded 333 origami cranes (a number that had special significance in the world of *Perplex City*), and a group of them personally delivered the cranes to Mind Candy's London office.

Characters die in fiction all the time, of course, and audiences are often devastated by it. But in this case, their grief was made deeper by the feeling that Anna was a friend, not just a character. After all, they'd read her website and seen puzzles she had designed for her children to solve. They'd emailed her, and she had responded to them.

Even worse, in the days leading up to her death, they had helped her to investigate a deadly secret society called the Third Power, and had even urged her to keep up her efforts. And, worst of all, they were the ones who had unwittingly sent her to her death that night.

They weren't merely sad—they felt personally responsible, because they had been complicit in her death. As Juxta on the online community Unfiction said, "That aching and seemingly bottomless little hole which has appeared, unbidden in the depths of your stomach as you heard this news? That would be guilt."

Any single-medium work can in theory make an audience laugh or cry. But make an audience feel directly involved in the events in a story? Whether we're talking about responsibility for sending a woman to her murder, or perhaps instead saving her life or introducing her to her future partner, you just can't evoke that feeling with a book or a movie.

This is the power of transmedia.

THE AUDIENCE EXPECTS MORE

If you're reading this book at all, you probably already know that transmedia is the hot new thing. Hollywood is buzzing about it. Madison Avenue is selling it. Film festivals are celebrating it. Audiences are consuming it, by the tens of millions. It is the realm of deep experiences and completely immersive stories, and it can evoke emotions that simply can't be replicated in a single novel or film.

Imagine Googling a fictional company from your favorite TV show and finding that it has a website. It turns out the company is hiring right now, so you apply for a job. A few days later, you get an email saying you've been hired.

Imagine calling up a security guard at the Statue of Liberty on the phone. You plead with him to rescue a friend of yours, a young boy who has been kidnapped and is being held close by. To your relief, the guard agrees to risk his job and help the boy; a life is saved.

Imagine taking to Twitter on Halloween to spin a story about H. P. Lovecraft's sanity-eroding Elder Gods returning to devour us all. And it's not just you—it's a joyful collaboration, with hundreds or even thousands of individuals fabricating a common fiction together.

All these things have happened in real transmedia projects, and that's just skimming the surface of what's possible. Transmedia is more than mere marketing or franchise entertainment. It's the realm of stories at the edge of where reality ends and fiction begins.

Once upon a time, nonfunctional phone numbers (555-0038) and fictional addresses (123 Main Street, Anytown, USA) were the de facto choice every creator made. Over time, audiences were trained out of their natural inclination to investigate further. They simply expected that any contact information in a story would be a dead end.

Today, though, that expectation has been overturned. If a character in a TV show hands out a business card, it's likely that you'll be treated to a close-up shot, including a working phone number, email address, or URL. Searching the web for fictional companies, places, and even characters is just as likely to turn up a website or social media profile as not. Email addresses mentioned in a show's dialogue will accept mail from you . . . and sometimes even write back. And when you add up all of these pieces, the whole is very much greater than the sum of its parts.

Creators have discovered that expanding their story universes to include these other components is feeding a core hunger of their truest fans: to have more, richer, deeper stories. Fans who love your creation are going to want to see more of it. They want to be a part of it. Transmedia—telling a story through multiple communication channels at once, particularly channels such as the web and social media—is the way to give them what they want.

BUSINESSES WANT MORE, TOO

Corporate heavy hitters like HBO, Disney, Sony Pictures, BBC, Warner Brothers, Ford, Scholastic, Penguin, and others have taken notice, and are spending more and more time and money on creating transmedia experiences. It's a topic of growing interest for independent artists, filmmakers, marketing execs, and TV and movie studios—and their jobs are increasingly depending on it.

The marketplace is already shifting fast to prepare for the new entertainment ecosystem to come in which transmedia is destined to play a crucial role.

In March 2011, transmedia received an enormous vote of confidence from the business establishment. Fourth Wall Studios, a small Los Angeles start-up specializing in transmedia entertainment, scored an investment round of $15 million, with access to a fund of $200 million more—a sum that would do any dot-com start-up proud. And that's just one news item following a long string of good news for trans-media creators.

That same month, no less than a dozen panels at the influential SXSW Interactive conference extolled the virtues of transmedia experiences. Looking back earlier in 2011, the ambitious transmedia film *Pandemic* took the Sundance Film Festival by storm, and tens of millions of people participated in the transmedia marketing campaign for *Tron: Legacy*, helping the film to rake in nearly $400 million worldwide.

Still further back, the film-focused Producers Guild of America introduced a transmedia producer credit in April 2010, legitimizing the title as its own credential. In 2009, the prestigious Grand Prix award at the Cannes Cyber Lions ad festival went to a transmedia narrative, *Why So Serious?*, a marketing campaign for *The Dark Knight*. And the International Emmys have given awards to interactive programs going back as far as 2006.

That's not even talking about the dozens of innovative and critically acclaimed independent projects.

But these events were a long time in coming. There is nothing sudden or unexpected about the widening interest in transmedia; it's just that the movement for transmedia storytelling is finally reaching a tipping point after years of buildup. Some creators have been working toward this moment for a decade and more. Now that the moment is here, the payoff is enormous.

There's money to be made and glory to be reaped. Creators who get into the transmedia game now will have an edge in the future. And if that's not enough to get your attention, you should know that transmedia opens up mind-blowing creative possibilities for artists, even those with limited budgets and tools. The world is your oyster.

And yet, despite all this interest—all these awards, press attention, and money—there is very little in the way of practical advice out there. Would-be creators are starving for information that can teach them not merely how to tap into digital media, but how to build compelling, well-executed transmedia projects that enhance the value and extend the reach of their properties.

This book can't be exhaustive, just as you can't draw a detailed map of undiscovered terrain. But I do have a lot of hard-won experience crafting transmedia stories; I've worked on marketing projects, original intellectual property (IP), and serious games. I've been commissioned, crowdfunded, and done client work. My projects have won awards ranging from the Vanguard Origins Innovation Award for game design to BIMAs to the Prix Jeunesse Interactivity Prize, and have even been nominated along the way for BAFTA and Games for Change awards.

I've picked up a few things along the way. *A Creator's Guide to Transmedia Storytelling* shares what I've learned with you.

Q&A: SEAN STEWART AND ELAN LEE

Sean Stewart and Elan Lee are two of the most innovative and widely known creators in transmedia. They were behind the alternate reality game for *A.I.* and helped to found 42 Entertainment, creating such hits as *ilovebees* for *Halo 2* and *Year Zero* for Nine Inch Nails. They have since moved on to found Fourth Wall Studios.

Q: *How did you get into transmedia?*

A: We started with a project for Steven Spielberg's movie *A.I.* The idea was to build out the world the movie was set in (Earth 2142), and then tell a story in it, spread out across web pages, emails, phone calls, live events, and even fax transmissions. (Remember fax machines?) I don't think any of us were thinking about the word *transmedia* at the time; we just wanted to bring you the story across every channel of your life.

That project, nicknamed *The Beast*, is now considered the first fully formed "alternate reality game" (ARG). From the day it launched, it was clear we had stumbled onto something kind of amazing. We've been working in the space ever since.

Q: *Can you tell me a little about your favorite projects?*

A: We're game designers and storytellers: our favorite moments are ones where the audience is delighted, astonished, moved, or amazed. In the early ARG work, it was incredible to see the power of a collective audience working together to uncover a story, as they did in *ilovebees*, going out to pay phones all over the world to collect a *War of the Worlds*–style radio drama about an alien invasion.

More recently, we've been working on making the tools of transmedia storytelling more accessible to a mainstream audience. In that regard, the fact that *Cathy's Book* (a transmedia novel) was an international bestseller was really gratifying. We set up our current shop, Fourth Wall Studios, to create these kinds of more accessible experiences. The very first thing we put out the door was called *Eagle Eye: Free Fall*. The day it came out, someone posted, "OMG I showed this to my mother-in-law and she LOVED it!" *That* was a huge win for us.

Q: *Where do you see the art and business of storytelling headed over the next few years?*

A: The Internet is a printing press, a movie camera. Just as those inventions led to the development of the novel and the motion picture, we're going to see the birth of new kinds of storytelling that are more than just "a book you read on your Kindle" or "a movie you watch on your iPad."

People will find ways to use the capabilities of the tech (the mic on your cell phone, the gyroscope on your tablet) to make you laugh and cry. And because spending all day on that is more fun than bagging groceries at the Piggly Wiggly, all of us who are interested in new forms of entertainment will be working hard to create the business models that support this next-gen content.

Q: *What would you recommend transmedia creators learn about to improve their craft?*

A: The audience.

Seriously, all the tech in the world is a means to an end, and the end is taking your audience somewhere amazing. If you're a writer, pay attention to writing that delights you. If you are a game designer, think about the games that you couldn't stop playing.

Then try keeping in mind a sort of Copernican revolution: instead of thinking of the entertainment as something that lives in a book (or box or console) that your audience has to come to, think of that audience as the sun: try building entertainment that orbits around them.

Q: *How has your design philosophy changed over the last 10 years?*

A: Well, we famously built our first project around the premise "This Is Not a Game." We wanted it to feel real, because we wanted the stakes to matter.

These days, we are every bit as dedicated to the idea that our stories should matter to people, but blurring the line between reality and fiction feels old. The world has caught up to transmedia. To use an analogy, people at the first motion pictures weren't sure that the train on the screen wasn't going to burst through the theater and run them down. But that moment passed in a heartbeat. Similarly, today's audiences are perfectly able to view everyday reality as something that can be "skinned" with a story as easily as they can change the wallpaper on their desktops.

Rather than ask them to believe that our content is "real," we just want to give them easy access to fascinating worlds and compelling characters.

Q: *Is there anything you wish you'd learned or tried earlier?*

A: From the very beginning, we've wanted to create original content, but in the early days, most of the exploration in this space was funded with marketing budgets. To be in a place where we spend time every day trying to create the iconic properties of the next generation of entertainment—*that's* exhilarating.

Q: *What advice would you give to an aspiring transmedia creator who's just starting out?*

A: Respect your audience. They deserve your best work.

When you are working, be prepared to iterate. Unless you are currently in the sixth grade, you grew up in a very different world, and your first ideas are going to come from an older paradigm. Be patient, but be relentless; the real treasure, the gold, is stuff you will discover in the process of creation, when you are at your wit's end and your first idea just isn't working.

And, of course, *good luck*!

2 What Is Transmedia, Anyway?

Before we can talk about how to make great transmedia projects, we have to clarify what we mean when we say "transmedia storytelling" (at least for the purposes of this book). This is shockingly difficult to do. For all of the excitement surrounding the word and its crackling aura of innovation, it's flat-out impossible to nail down a single definition that everyone can happily agree on.

There's a divide between what some wags call West Coast versus East Coast transmedia. West Coast-style transmedia, more commonly called Hollywood or franchise transmedia, consists of multiple big pieces of media: feature films, video games, that kind of thing. It's grounded in big-business commercial storytelling. The stories in these projects are interwoven, but lightly; each piece can be consumed on its own, and you'll still come away with the idea that you were given a complete story.

A great example of this would be *Star Wars*, where multiple films, books, TV series, and so on combine to tell the long-ago history of a galaxy far, far away. Both new franchises, like *Avatar*, and reboots of old ones, like *Tron* and *Transformers*, are increasingly embracing this approach.

On the other end of the spectrum, East Coast transmedia tends to be more interactive, and much more web-centric. It overlaps heavily with the traditions of independent film, theater, and interactive art. These projects make heavy use of social media, and are often run once over a set period of time rather than persisting forever. The plot is so tightly woven between media that you might not fully understand what's going on if you don't actively seek out multiple pieces of the story.

For our example here, consider Lance Weiler's indie film experience *Pandemic*, which incorporated a live scavenger hunt, a short film, comics, Twitter feeds, and more, all unfolding at the Sundance Film Festival over a few action-packed days.

If the term *transmedia* means anything at all, how can *Star Wars* and *Pandemic* both be transmedia at the same time?

A LITTLE BACKSTORY

To answer that, let's back up and review the history: The term *transmedia* was originally coined by cultural theorist and University of Southern California professor Dr. Marsha Kinder. She first used it in 1991 as "transmedia intertextuality," describing works where characters appeared across multiple media, like the Teenage Mutant Ninja Turtles (what we would generally call an entertainment franchise these days).

Dr. Henry Jenkins, a media theorist who was then at MIT but is now at USC, has brought transmedia to popular attention in recent years, most notably through his book *Convergence Culture*. He reframed Kinder's term to describe heavily integrated narratives like *The Matrix*. In that narrative, the different media components—films, video games, a graphic novel—are so intertwined that a character can walk offstage in the game and appear in the film in his very next breath.

This is the definition Jenkins has posted on his blog, "Confessions of an Aca-Fan":

> Transmedia storytelling represents a process where integral elements of a fiction get *dispersed systematically across multiple delivery channels* for the purpose of creating *a unified and coordinated entertainment experience*. Ideally, each medium makes its own *unique contribution* to the unfolding of the story. [Emphasis his, not mine.]

Thus, we have three criteria for transmedia storytelling: multiple media, a single unified story or experience, and avoidance of redundancy between media. Sounds like *Star Wars* to me. Sounds like *Pandemic*, too. But if transmedia storytelling is the process that results in both of these kinds of structures, what exactly are you doing in that process?

FRAGMENTATION

Telling a story transmedia-style involves one of two processes, actually. Either you take a single story and you splinter it across multiple media, or you start with one story and you keep adding pieces on to it *ad infinitum*. Both of these processes will result in projects that can be described with phrases like "greater than the sum of its parts" and "a single cohesive story."

There is a point of similarity in both techniques, though; a meaningful underlying commonality. The end result of both processes is fragmentation—the story has been broken into pieces. It's just a matter of scale. *Star Wars* uses a story that's been broken into really big fragments (a whole film, a book), and *Pandemic* uses much smaller ones (a single bottle of water, a series of tweets). And then there are a number of hybrid projects that mix big and little pieces together, like *Cathy's Book*, which used a single-medium narrative piece (a book), but combined it with fragments of evidence and online components to tell a deeper story.

The transmedia fragmentation spectrum

No matter how big the pieces are, though, you interact with them using the same basic behavior. Compare this with different kinds of jigsaw puzzles. There are five-thousand-piece jigsaw puzzles out there, and if you pick up only one piece, you can't guess whether the whole thing will be a mountaintop or a potted plant. There are also simpler puzzles where each piece looks like an entire horse or cow or sheep, but as with more complex puzzles, you still have to finish the puzzle to see the whole farm.

Of course, the more pieces you break a story into, the more likely it is that you're going to be entering a highly distributed structure and embedding pieces of story into the real world. You're more likely to be using interactive elements and real-time platforms. This is what makes for sexy, award-winning marketing campaigns and deep, immersive experiences.

I'll admit my biases up front: This kind of highly fragmented narrative is where I get my thrills. This is where you find writing-as-performance-art. It's where you find audience-as-agent. This is the thing that gets me excited about the power of transmedia.

And—to get back to the business of creation—it's also a more educational subject to study, if you're at all interested in transmedia storytelling, because the tricks and tools of single-medium storytelling won't serve you very well. Big-business transmedia narratives using tentpole feature films, AAA video games, and books from the Big Six publishing firms can be integrated into unified story universes without shifting into a completely transmedia mindset. But if you learn how to create a highly fragmented narrative, that knowledge will serve you no matter where on the spectrum you land.

QUESTIONS ALL THE WAY DOWN

Transmedia as it's commonly known today is storytelling on the cusp of new possibilities. We'll probably see skirmishes over what transmedia means and whether any given project is transmedia at all for years to come, as those possibilities grow and change.

But that doesn't really matter much. The important thing isn't that we all settle on a definition that will endure through the ages. There is nothing wrong with the debate continuing, as long as we creators in the trenches keep trying a lot of different structures, tools, and innovations.

Jenkins himself worries that we have "too much focus on the definitional and not on the analytic." We're focusing on whether something is or isn't technically transmedia, when we might be much better off examining the field of prior art to see where and how various pieces work. "A lot of hybrid things are emerging that are difficult to classify," he said.

That's exactly the way it should be. Don't worry about whether or not your project is technically going to be transmedia. Worry about making it something people will care about.

WHAT'S IN A NAME?

There may continue to be some scuffling about definitions for some time to come, because a lot of money and credibility could ride on the outcome. The history of the transmedia producer credit is a case in point.

When the Producers Guild of America first announced that it was creating a transmedia producer credit, this immediately caused quite a bit of controversy. That's because the PGA's definition is "three stories told via three distinct media." The PGA has a list of what qualifies as a distinct medium, too, including television broadcasts and feature films.

WORDS WE CAN'T USE

There are a number of words we can't use in place of *transmedia*, because they already mean something very specific, or else they exclude one of the kinds of projects that you would call transmedia.

Multimedia

On the surface, *multimedia* sounds like it describes exactly what transmedia is meant to be: multiple media. Unfortunately, in the 1990s, the term took on a very specific connotation: text, video, audio, and images delivered together through computer. Multimedia CD-ROMs of atlases and encyclopedias were common and profitable for a few years. They vanished when the new king of the multimedia experience arose: the World Wide Web.

Interactive Fiction

You might think a story that you can interact with is interactive fiction. But this phrase has been taken for decades to mean a very specific kind of computer game: the text adventure, as in games like *Zork* or *Moonmist*. These were the particular specialty of a Massachusetts company named Infocom, which was taken over by Activision in 1986.

But there's another reason why transmedia storytelling can't be called interactive fiction, and that's the growing interest in transmedia documentaries and serious games. The same tools you can use for telling a story that isn't true can just as easily be used to call attention to real-world information.

Cross-Media

Until very recently, *cross-media* was the top contender to mean the same thing as transmedia. Now, a consensus is growing that cross-media refers to releasing the same content (like, say, a TV show) over multiple platforms. So cross-media is what lets you see the same episode of *Yo Gabba Gabba* on TV, on your phone, and on a DVD.

Alternate Reality Game (ARG)

An alternate reality game is a social media narrative that plays out in real time, using real communications media to make it seem as though the story were really happening. Sounds a lot like transmedia, right? And in fact the ARG is a subset of transmedia—*Perplex City* was an ARG. But the accepted formula for an ARG requires elements that a transmedia project doesn't always have, such as direct communication with characters or puzzles for the players to solve.

Indie creators like Dr. Christy Dena and Brooke Thompson expressed concern that this would freeze out some kinds of projects that feel like transmedia, but don't meet the three-media rule, or those where multiple media are telling a single plot line, not three distinct stories.

At the same time, groups like the PGA have no choice but to create a clear and objective definition for what transmedia means in order to decide who can qualify for their credit. The PGA isn't the only example, either. Funding bodies like the Tribeca Film Festival must offer definitions to spell out who can qualify for grant money—and who can't.

That means that any definition for *transmedia* is genuinely high-stakes. It's not just an intellectual fencing match; whether or not you can put "PGA transmedia producer" on your résumé could be a career changer. But once you've drawn a line, inevitably a deserving project or creator will be on the wrong side of it.

The definition has proven to be a moving target so far, making everything just a little more complicated. It's already difficult to keep track of the novel ways in which creators are telling immersive stories today. It's dead impossible to foresee the innovations in storytelling that new technology and new visionaries will give us in 5, 10, or 15 years.

So it might take decades for the dust to settle. But there's no sense in waiting for consensus on a complete definition before you start making something amazing yourself. There's a lot of territory to explore, and it's going to be just as much fun no matter what words we use to label our work.

3

Transmedia Is More Than a Marketing Gimmick

*I*t's all well and good to address what transmedia is, but I'd also like to talk about something that transmedia is not. There is a misperception that transmedia storytelling is nothing but a marketing tool—a gimmick, even. This is an understandable mistake, but it's a mistake all the same.

One of the early milestones of transmedia was a marketing campaign for the film *A.I.* The marketing campaign is now known as *The Beast*, and it spawned an online community called the Cloudmakers that over time evolved to become the modern alternate reality game community.

Cloudmaker and transmedia creator Jay Bushman has likened *The Beast* and its lasting influence to *Birth of a Nation*, a now-controversial film released in 1915. *Birth of a Nation* wasn't the first film to use many of the techniques that it used, but it was the first to stitch them into a whole that demonstrated how powerful they could be when used in conjunction.

**A 1915 movie poster for
*Birth of a Nation***

Likewise, *The Beast* was by no means the first time anyone created a fictional website or blogged as a made-up character. And it definitely wasn't the project that invented the technique of creating evidence of a story and playing it out as though it were really happening. (The roots of this narrative style are older than the Internet, older even than electricity, sunk deep in the tradition of epistolary novels—arguably invented in Spain in the thirteenth century.) But it integrated all these elements into a whole that suddenly set a new bar for storytelling.

The Beast was undoubtedly meant to be marketing. But to players, it didn't feel like marketing at all. It seemed much more like one piece with the film—a single work telling just one sprawling and complex story.

The Blair Witch Project hit the scene at about the same time. For 15 years, *Blair Witch* reigned as the most profitable independent film of all time; it remains a cultural touchstone even now. *Blair Witch*'s famous extended experience included the same kinds of complementary narrative we now see everywhere.

Blair Witch filmmaker Mike Monello is a marketer today, and a co-founder of Campfire Media. Monello is proud of what he does (as well he should be, given the work he's done for HBO, Discovery, and other clients). He has no reason to shy away from calling the *Blair Witch* extended experience a clever marketing campaign; quite the reverse, in fact, since it turned out to be a brilliant factor in the film's success. And still, he is adamant that the extended world they created was more than a marketing ploy.

"*The Blair Witch Project* experience was never intended as a marketing campaign. The mythology, in fact, was created before the film was shot and was used as a shared history for the actors to improvise from about the *Blair Witch*," Monello said. "When we began building the online experience, the film wasn't even finished, so we had nothing to market. For all of us it was much more about building fans than about straight-up marketing, and I think that's why the story endures today when most marketing narratives quickly fade from consciousness."

And yet transmedia storytelling and marketing are intertwined in people's heads. The tendency to call a transmedia experience a marketing campaign if there is an intended monetary transaction at any point is surprisingly common. *Perplex City* was an online fictional universe that was free to consume, but it included a series of related collectible puzzle cards that were available for sale. Consumers could just follow the story or just buy the cards, but the experience was more rewarding if you did both. And yet I've heard people say that, for example, "*Perplex City* was marketing, it was just marketing itself."

This is ludicrous. It's like saying all cinema is created as a marketing tool for selling theater tickets. Yes, there are films where, sadly, that's not too far off the mark, but it entirely misses the entire medium of film as an art form. Same with transmedia.

VISIBILITY

So why do we have this idea that transmedia equals marketing floating around, anyway? Just off the top of my head, I can cite a dozen transmedia stories that can't be called marketing in any sense, starting with my own projects: the independent collectible card-game-plus-immersive-fiction *Perplex City*; the Channel 4 educational docudrama *Routes*; the human-rights-driven *America 2049*, created with the nonprofit group Breakthrough.

Branching out from my own portfolio, you see lighthearted indie works like *Must Love Robots*, the story of a robot searching for love in Brooklyn; the bestselling *Cathy's Book* series by Sean Stewart, which includes photographs, phone numbers to call, and websites to visit; the *lonelygirl15* web series, which let audience members talk to a home-schooled girl and let her talk back to them; indie transmedia films like Lance Weiler's *Head Trauma* and the live-event-driven *Pandemic*; and the serious game *World Without Oil*, which encouraged people to imagine living on the other side of the energy apocalypse.

Why don't these projects get the same kind of mainstream mindshare? That comes down to economics. It's not that there are more marketing campaigns that use

transmedia tools than there are original and indie works; it's that the marketing campaigns are much, much more visible. Why? Because they have more money to throw around.

For one thing, they're a lot more likely to be able to pay the team a living wage, which means the creators can afford to devote more time and care to the project instead of working only in their off hours and on weekends. More money means higher production values; dollars spent translate pretty well into better-looking video, better-sounding audio, and sleeker, glossier websites. Audiences like that. (And why shouldn't they?)

Even more important than having improved production values, money lets you promote the story. This is crucial: you need to pull people into your project. The most effective means of promotion are any traditional media you can afford: TV spots, billboards, bus shelters, whatever. There may be a day when that changes, but it's not here yet. It's even better if you can hire a great publicist to pitch your project to *Wired*, *Variety*, the *Guardian*, and the *New York Times*, too.

This is why the most successful transmedia projects to date (as measured by number of participants) have, by and large, been part of an overarching marketing campaign. Those folks can afford to promote the project. And transmedia projects need promoting, just like every other form of entertainment does.

That's not to say that transmedia storytelling has nothing to offer marketers. Millions of dollars and millions of eyeballs would both disagree with that! But the long-term benefits of transmedia marketing are not in drawing in a completely new audience, but in hooking a peripheral audience more deeply and keeping it around longer. It's that magic word: engagement.

And even marketers might want to keep their eyes on where transmedia storytelling may go in the future. After all, marketing dollars have done a lot to shape transmedia storytelling; but as Bushman says, vaudeville marketing dollars did a lot to shape early cinema, too. Vaudeville incorporated movies into its shows as early as 1902. It was widely considered a marketing gimmick at the time.

By 1932, though, New York's premiere vaudeville venue, the Palace Theatre, had switched to all movies all the time. Cinema is a lot bigger than vaudeville now, to say the least. Not bad for something that started out as marketing, huh? Give us transmedia creators that same hundred years and we'll wind up a lot bigger than just a marketing technique, too.

4
Significant Prior Art to Learn From

*T*ransmedia has hit broad mainstream attention only in the last few years, but there is already a rich body of prior art. Creators have told stories in a breathtaking number of ways, and the tools of transmedia have been used for an enormous variety of purposes.

The wise creator should spend some time becoming familiar with projects that have gone before, how those projects were structured, and how the audience reacted to them. You can learn quite a lot about what to do and what to avoid in your own work. We'll take a quick glance at a few influential and innovative projects here, but you'd be well advised to research them on your own, too. I can only give you a taste of what's out there, but there's a whole buffet within your grasp, if you just reach for it.

MARKETING CAMPAIGNS

Naturally, many of the most notable transmedia stories of the last decade (give or take a couple of years) have been marketing campaigns—particularly for films.

As previously noted, the two campaigns that are most widely regarded as representing the birth of transmedia marketing are the *A.I.* game (also known as *The Beast*) and *The Blair Witch Project*. Both of them used online resources in order to expand on the world and the story set forth in their respective films.

The Beast, which is generally considered the first alternate reality game (ARG), enthralled people with four months of puzzles, emails, and increasingly richer glimpses into the world of the movie. The game turned a fire hose of content on its audience: constantly updating websites, emails from characters, puzzles set by a mysterious Japanese businessman, and codes from the robot revolutionary underground. Players attended Anti-Robot Militia rallies, cracked Enigma ciphers, and interpreted lute tablature along the way.

Most of the characters in the film weren't in the game, and in fact the game was set many years after the end of the film. The primary exception was Martin Swinton, a minor but very significant character who is a child in the film *A.I.* In *The Beast*, he grapples with the events from the movie, now that he is a grown man.

Indeed, the game worked on two levels: as an independent mystery, in which the players tried to help a young woman solve the murder of her friend Evan Chan; and as a study in the long-term consequences of the events of the film. It's no surprise that the game's writer, Sean Stewart, is also an award-winning novelist.

According to Dr. Christy Dena's compilation of ARG statistics, the game drew between 1 and 3 million players from around the world, and created more than 300 million impressions from coverage in mainstream media: *Wired*, *CNN*, *Time* magazine, and so on.

The Blair Witch Project went down a different path, presenting a unified appearance that the film was a real documentary about three hikers who go missing in the woods. The film's website included a timeline of the story's mythology, fictional evidence from an investigation of the events in the film, and even made-up credentials for the filmmakers, all presented in as realistic and authentic a way as possible.

Audiences took this material at face value (at least initially), and the campaign topped lists of the top web hoaxes of all time for several years. It was widely reported on as a hoax in mainstream media. And it was a tremendous success; the campaign is often credited with making *Blair Witch* one of the most profitable independent films of all time—a reported $248 million for a film that cost less than $1 million to make.

Transmedia tools have also been used to market the films *The Dark Knight, District 9, 2012, Tron: Legacy, Cloverfield, Salt, The International, Eagle Eye*, and on and on. Often these campaigns have competition tie-ins to give out prizes. But the most important element is that each of them brings something to the audience that wasn't conveyed in the film.

As an example, *Why So Serious?,* the immersive marketing campaign that 42 Entertainment created for *The Dark Knight*, acted as a direct prequel to the movie. This allowed audiences to walk into theaters already familiar with many of the characters and dynamics, particularly those surrounding the election of Gotham City district attorney candidate Harvey Dent.

The game's audience was even the Joker's accomplice in the theft of a school bus that the Joker uses to make his getaway in the opening moments of the film. This created an instant connection between the two pieces, and made those in the audience suddenly feel like they had been a part of something greater than themselves—that they had a direct and very personal connection to the movie. The campaign created a situation where small elements of the film felt like a big payoff to the audience.

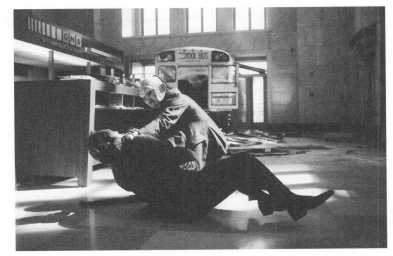

The Joker's getaway vehicle—a yellow school bus
The Dark Knight *(2008). Used by permission of Warner Bros. Entertainment Inc.*

OTHER MEDIA

When transmedia marketing moves into television, you see a subtle shift in the relationship between transmedia components and the main event; the chronologies begin to overlap. For the NBC show *Heroes*, for example, the online *Heroes 360 Experience* provided a wealth of complementary content, including a web comic that spelled out many characters' origins and motivations, sometimes before they even appeared on the show. The *360 Experience* players were already well familiar with the character of Wireless, for example, long before she walked onscreen.

Players even had the chance to apply for a job at Primatech Paper, a cover organization in the show for a group of hero hunters. Most of this online content provided extra exposition shedding light on the events and intrigues of the show, though, rather than expanding the main storyline.

Heroes is by no means alone in its techniques; shows from *Lost* to *The Office* to *How I Met Your Mother* have built great transmedia extensions. We'll look at these in a little more detail in the discussion of worldbuilding in the next chapter.

Other kinds of media have started using transmedia tools to market and engage, as well. The video game *Halo 2* had one of the most notable transmedia marketing campaigns of all time in *ilovebees*, not to mention the *Halo* franchise's successful foray into publishing. Other games since then that have used transmedia tools to sell to or expand their audience include *Portal*, *Assassin's Creed*, *Dragon Age*, and *Tomb Raider: Underworld*.

Even musicians have gotten into the act. The bands Gorillaz and Nine Inch Nails, Swedish performer Jonna Lee, and pop musician Thomas Dolby have all created transmedia stories that integrate with and expand upon their music.

The Primatech Paper website
NBCU Photo Bank. Used with permission.

But while transmedia marketing is a natural step for media companies that are already all about storytelling, these companies aren't the only game in town. Increasingly, nonmedia brands are using transmedia storytelling as marketing, too. Audi's *Art of the Heist* campaign had players searching for stolen Audi A3s along with a retrieval business for stolen works of art. In its wake, we've seen transmedia campaigns from Toyota (*Your Other You*), Ford (the *Ford Focus Rally*), and Mazda (*33 Keys*). And it hasn't been just automakers—similar storytelling tools have been used for brands as diverse as Levi's jeans, the perfume Covet, the beer Stella Artois, and Old Spice's line of men's personal care products.

Given the scope and success of these projects, it's easy to see why transmedia and marketing get along so famously.

ORIGINAL TRANSMEDIA NARRATIVES

But again, don't forget that transmedia is a lot bigger than just marketing. There are a growing number of commercial and indie projects that are transmedia entertainment, even in the absence of transmedia marketing.

The most widely known examples are the big-budget franchises, like *Star Wars* and *The Matrix*. These high-profile commercial franchises are considered transmedia storytelling because they include an element of intertextuality. That means that a single story thread plays out over more than one medium. The romance between Princess Leia and Han Solo starts on film, for example, but it continues in the books. You'd need to switch media to follow the course of their relationship and how it plays out.

That's not to say that every entertainment franchise is transmedia. That's very much not the case! Franchises where the different media only replay the same story (like a novelization of a film), or where the different media aren't related to one another beyond a common logo or name, just don't have the key hallmarks of transmedia.

Franchise-style transmedia storytelling is fairly common and becoming more so, but creators should also be aware of the enormous body of original, more highly fragmented transmedia stories out there. You'll find an incredible variety of structures and revenue models.

Nowadays, most original, nonmarketing transmedia projects feature a tentpole video element, be that a film, a TV show, or a web series. Take, for example, the popular MTV show *Valemont*, which consisted of shows played on the air and a sprawling, highly interactive social media footprint for the characters. This vampire university show was so successful that a second season is reported to be in the works; Electric Farm Entertainment has sold the show to international markets, as well.

Valemont is arguably the logical next step from older projects like *lonelygirl15*, which in turn owes much to *Blair Witch*. The *lonelygirl15* web series about a home-schooled girl video blogging at first gave the appearance of being for real, but over time it evolved into an alternate reality game that included characters who interacted with the audience online, real-world events, and even product placement. Unlike most original transmedia stories these days, it was impossible to tell from the outset that *lonelygirl15* was fiction. (This was a popular method through the mid-2000s, but it is falling out of favor as concerns about liability and creation of sustainable fan bases take center stage.)

Other transmedia projects a creator should be aware of include independent films like filmmaker Lance Weiler's *Pandemic* project, discussed later in Chapter 23. This project might be called a short film, but that understates the breadth and scope of a project that included an installation of an "abandoned car" at the Sundance Film Festival, a stunning technical build that let the audience learn about the fictional victims of the titular pandemic in a touch-sensitive table, and a three-day scavenger hunt for bottles of water, gold items, and gadget-laden bears made of a mucuslike material.

Moving past video-centric projects, creators should also study *Jejune Institute*, a lushly produced locative fiction project. *Jejune Institute* incorporated real-world art objects into ordinary spaces in a San Francisco neighborhood, shaping a narrative that small groups could walk through in just a few hours. This project was created by Nonchalance, a marketing company, without an intent for a return on investment, but a similar model could easily be used as a marketing tool for local business groups, or even as a for-pay experience at hotels or other leisure destinations.

Consumer goods and entertainment experiences aren't the only things being sold by transmedia. We've seen a growing body of serious games—that is, games that aim to be fun, but also to call attention to big-picture serious issues like the energy crisis, human rights, or poverty. In short, serious games are marketing ideals and ideas.

World Without Oil was one of the first big serious games meant to incite positive real-world change among its participants. The project invited players to create content as though they were living in a post-Peak Oil world together. Players described the social and economic changes they imagined might take place. Other serious games to scrutinize important real-world issues include *Conspiracy for Good, Urgent Evoke*, and my own *America 2049*.

HYBRID PROJECTS

There is a temptation for us transmedia professionals to step in and take credit every time a new and innovative story crosses our path. But just as not all serial narrative is transmedia, not every cool or interactive or social or compelling story experience is transmedia, either. Still, there is a significant gray area, and some of these hybrid projects can be just as worthy of examination for best practices as any other source.

One example is *Sleep No More*, a critically acclaimed theater performance by Punchdrunk, which has so far been shown in London, Boston, and New York. It's a reimagining of Shakespeare's *Macbeth*. During the show, the audience is dispersed across five floors of a "hotel," each representing a different place in the story world: a mist-wreathed graveyard with an iron fence; a loud nightclub; a row of bathtubs in an insane asylum. The audience must wander through these locations, sometimes stumbling on actors and watching the scenes play out, as though they have become particularly voyeuristic ghosts. Just performance art, right? Yes—until you learn that the show extends into some puzzle-driven bonus material similar to an ARG. Transmedia or not? Hard to say.

And there is a whole genre of Twitter fiction, like the works of Jay Bushman, called "the epic poet of Twitter" by *New Scientist*. He's done a number of works under the banner of The Loose-Fish Project, notably Twitter dramas like *#SXStarWars*, *Cthalloween*, and *The Talking Dead*.

Cthalloween was a collaborative Twitter fiction project for Halloween of 2009. Participants visited the project's main website to choose an archetype to play as: The Questing Professor, The Tormented Artist, The Suspicious Citizen, or The Gibbering Cultist. Each had a timeline describing what kind of events should take place at what point over the course of the night. And then it was in the hands of the audience: participants used their personal Twitter accounts to tell the story of their own fictional experiences on the night when Lovecraft's Elder Gods awaken. Because these threads were synchronized by that single timeline, the result was a complete tapestry of many small fictions, combining to make something greater. Do multiple streams of content on the same platform count as multiple media, or not?

And then, of course, there are projects that behave in a fragmented fashion, even if the experience stays within a single frame. Mobile applications like *Urban Sleuth*, for example, and the online experience *Eagle Eye: Free Fall* have taken steps toward this kind of structure: single-player and replayable at any time, but still creating a feeling of immersion and authenticity, as if the experience is actually occurring. There is a massive benefit to this approach: it's reducing the moments of risk where an audience member has to switch to another medium to continue the story, but might choose to just walk away instead. If a game feels like it's using video clips, instant messaging, and email, but it's all really happening in a single bespoke application and is a single platform under the hood, is it transmedia, or isn't it?

Let's not get bogged down in the definitional. There is something to learn even from projects at the periphery of transmedia storytelling: structures that work, best practices, framing and promotional techniques. Learn from everything you can; there's no need to worry about how to label it at all.

Q&A: MICHAEL ANDERSEN

Michael Andersen is a longtime journalist and critic within the transmedia community. He runs the site ARGN.com, an unmissable resource for news and analysis of alternate reality games, with coverage frequently extending into transmedia, pervasive stories, and viral marketing efforts.

Q: *How did you get into transmedia?*

A: My first exposure to transmedia was a Japanese film called *All About Lily Chou-Chou*. The film was about the fans of a fictional pop idol, Lily Chou-Chou. To get around a creative block he was facing in writing the film, Shunji Iwai created the website Lilyholic.com as a space for his characters to work through the mystery of a murder at Shibuya Quarter. Fans became entranced with the demo tracks of Lily's music as well as the online story that unfolded on this fictional fan site, and I became fascinated with the idea of creating these alternate realities that create layers of meaning to the world around us.

Q: *Can you tell me a little about your favorite projects?*

A: One of my favorite projects was *Chain Factor*, an alternate reality game created by area/code to expand on the narrative started in an episode of the CBS program *Numb3rs* featuring rogue game developers. Players were asked to locate hidden messages in billboards, television commercials, and websites to unlock abilities in an online flash game. Error codes peppered throughout the game provided hints at the events that transpired during the episode that kicked off the game in the first place.

I'm also partial to an alternate reality game that Jasper Fforde launched for his novel *First Among Sequels*. In Fforde's Thursday Next books, the lines between literature and the real world are blurred. Fictional characters are self-aware, and they share the ability to jump between worlds with real people. For the project, Jasper Fforde's real-world book tour was threatened by a fictional version of himself who was attempting to supplant the real Fforde and release a bastardized version of *First Among Sequels*.

Both of these projects created situations where the incorporation of transmedia elements was an organic extension of the story world.

Q: *Where do you see the art and business of storytelling headed over the next few years?*

A: For the past few years of transmedia storytelling, revenue models have been centered around getting people to pay for tangible goods. EDOC Laundry asked players to purchase T-shirts to unlock content, *Perplex City* and *39 Clues* tied their revenue to collectible cards, and Wrigley's *5 gum* is currently requiring players to purchase packs of gum to advance in the story. While this commodification of storytelling will no doubt continue, I expect to see a resurgence in models that focus on monetizing the experiences themselves.

Q: *What would you recommend that transmedia creators learn about to improve their craft?*

A: Play games, and voraciously consume the media you plan on using. I find it hard to trust a chef who won't taste his own cooking as he prepares a meal. Often, the elements of projects that resonate with people who are actively participating in campaigns are not the ones that are featured in press releases and case studies featuring successful implementations. If you find you don't have enough time to delve into these projects, realize that your prospective audience might be similarly limited and plan accordingly.

Q: *What projects stand out as the best examples to learn from on what to do—and what not to do?*

A: The best examples of transmedia projects to learn from are either currently running or replayable, since the best instruction is firsthand experience. Patrick

Carman's *Skeleton Creek* series of books shows how text and video can be wedded organically to create a hauntingly authentic story, while the *Accomplice* series of interactive theater performances in New York, Los Angeles, and London provides instruction on how to guide players through a story while still making them feel part of it.

Q: *Do you see any trends emerging in what makes a successful project?*

A: With transmedia projects in particular, it's extremely tempting to get wrapped up in worldbuilding, ensuring that the alternate reality that you craft is as authentic as possible. However, players are unlikely to interact with your world, no matter how elaborate it is, unless the world is populated by vibrant characters that are central to the experience. When players describe their favorite transmedia projects, it's invariably about their favorite characters. When those characters are put in danger, player creativity and engagement generally spike dramatically.

Q: *Is there anything you see that keeps on getting tried, even though it never works?*

A: It's often tempting to pit players against one another, encouraging them to join factions and work against each other. However, doing so invariably causes online discussions to migrate to private forums, making it harder to expand the audience, as newcomers are regarded with suspicion and information is hoarded.

Transmedia projects may also try to hoax their players, attempting to convince players that an aspect of their fictional universe is actually real. This leads players to grow increasingly confused about the boundaries between the game world and the real world, which often derails the intended narrative.

AN AUDIENCE BY ANY OTHER NAME . . .

Throughout this book, I use a lot of different words to refer to transmedia projects. Since "transmedia story" gets a little clunky on repetition, I'll often talk about these projects in terms of a story, as a game, as a performance, or as a world, interchanging the terms freely. I also use several different words to refer to the people who are going to be engaging with your content. They're audience, players, users, fans, consumers, or participants.

Unfortunately, each one of these words has some resonance with its single-medium predecessors. But don't be deceived; just because I'm referring to a project as a game (because my background is very game-centric) and calling the people it's aimed at players (because ditto) doesn't mean that I'm not talking about something you should learn from, even if you're not making anything you could call a game. You should pay attention all the same.

One of the strengths of the transmedia toolbox is that we can all hone our craft by taking advantage of the hard-won lessons of those who have come before us. We don't have to reinvent theater, and if we're transplanting a live theatrical performance onto a livestream feed, well, we can all learn a lot from looking at how theater production works. Likewise, we can learn a great deal about interactivity from games, and we can perfect our written materials or spoken dialogue by reading everything we can about the craft of writing novels, scripts, and plays.

But as a side effect of that crazy interdisciplinary stew, terminology gets a little muddled. These long-separate communities of creators have each come up with lots of different words that all mean basically the same thing in the end. And the new community of creators is so busy making exciting stuff that we haven't yet had the time or need to come to a consensus on what-that's-called-in-transmedia.

Don't worry, you'll get the hang of it in no time.

SECTION II

STORYTELLING

5

The Four Creative Purposes for Transmedia Storytelling

Now let's forget all about buzz, all about definitions, and all about what's been done, and finally turn our attention to the juicy affair of why and how to use transmedia tools to tell your story. There are several compelling reasons to go transmedia, and these primarily fall into two basic camps: the business case and your creative vision.

For media companies, the business case is actually quite simple. Transmedia storytelling can provide more engagement and more potential points of sale for any given story, and when it's done well, each piece can effectively become a promotional tool pointing toward every other piece of the whole.

This should be fairly intuitive. Think about the huge number of fans who read the Harry Potter books and were desperate to see the movie—a phenomenon that was also seen with *Lord of the Rings*, *Game of Thrones*, *True Blood*, *Twilight*, and others. Nobody is arguing that *Lord*

Star Wars, the benchmark for franchise transmedia

of the Rings is a transmedia narrative, but this clearly demonstrates that when fans really love a story, they're willing to spend a lot of time and money for the privilege of staying in that universe as long as possible.

For all the complaints about Hollywood making too many sequels and not enough original works, if the audiences didn't want to spend millions of dollars watching those sequels, they'd never get made.

The business case for going transmedia grows even stronger when you look at long-running entertainment empires like *Star Wars*. The history of the *Star Wars* universe now plays out through hundreds of films, books, and comics; an animated TV series; and video games. As the appeal and the cultural resonance of *Star Wars* became more soundly established, Lucasfilm was able to use its intellectual property to license or create products ranging from action figures and playsets to sheets, swimsuits, and even Pez dispensers.

The value of the *Star Wars* franchise is hard to measure (Lucasfilm is a privately held company and doesn't disclose financial information), but according to analysts, the sky isn't even the limit.

For marketing consumer goods, the business case is a little more complicated because there generally isn't a core story already in existence that can be extended; however, it's all about creating an opportunity for engagement—making a story that your consumers care about will give them a positive association with your brand. This is the basic tenet that the modern advertising industry is built on. (We'll talk about story and branding at further length in a few chapters.)

But the business case isn't enough. Audiences don't like entertainment that feels like nothing but a grab for their hard-earned cash; they need to feel like there is an equitable transaction in place. It's the same thing with transmedia. If you want to succeed, you shouldn't just be bolting on a few components because they're what the industry thinks is sexy right now. You need to have a creative purpose for each piece, and you have to be acutely aware of how all the pieces fit together to make a whole that is bigger than the sum of its parts.

Let me say that again for emphasis: every single element of a transmedia story has to be fulfilling a narrative purpose, without exception.

If you don't also have an underlying creative function for each piece, then the project you make will fall flat, fans will complain, and all those riches to be earned through building a transmedia empire with a robust fan base will not be yours after all.

Following are the most common creative purposes and methods for expanding a single-medium story, either by using transmedia tools or by transforming it into a full-blown, natively transmedia world.

WORLDBUILDING

If you're just beginning to wade into transmedia storytelling, you might want to start out in the shallow end of the pool, so to speak. Assuming that you're creating a single-platform story and thinking about building out just one or two transmedia pieces, the place to begin is with simple worldbuilding.

Worldbuilding is all about efficiently conveying information about the time, place, and mood of your story. In cinema, the equivalent might be an establishing shot: the quick sweep over the grounds of the high school before a scene starts in a classroom, for example, or the flyover of the Eiffel Tower to convey that the characters are in Paris.

In a text-only work of fiction, like a novel, you would use descriptive language and telling details, perhaps describing the clothes people are wearing, the architecture and building materials of a town, the weather or lighting, or the smells and sounds, to make a setting come to life in the mind's eye.

In transmedia storytelling, though, the most effective tool is to actually create a small piece of your world and give it to your audience to play with.

This piece of the world is often online—this is the realm of the oft-used fictional corporate websites, for example. *Wall-E*'s Buy n Large (a sort of satirized version of Walmart) had a web presence when the film was launched, where you could "shop" for different kinds of robots. This allowed the future viewer to explore parts of the *Wall-E* universe that weren't in the movie at all or, better, to learn more about robots that were on screen only briefly (and hence learn more about the world they inhabited.)

The Maester's Path marketing campaign for the HBO series *Game of Thrones* was all worldbuilding, in a more literal sense than usual—Campfire Media created a series of "sensory experiences" that evoked the world of *Game of Thrones*, but didn't convey anything about the plot or the characters. (In the spirit of full disclosure, I had the pleasure of working on this project.) The campaign sent a select few bloggers gorgeous chests filled with aromatherapy-like kits, each meant to provide the scent of a particular location in the show. So the Crossroads Inn, a busy pub on two major roads, was represented by the aromas of crusty bread baking on the hearth, the wooden beams the inn was built from, and an imported pear brandy for the inn's higher-class patrons.

Game of Thrones scent chest
Copyright Campfire Media. Used with permission.

The Maester's Path also included an online audio experience that created the feeling that you were walking around the public room of that inn and eavesdropping on the conversations of its patrons and staff; later, it added food carts in New York and Los Angeles where fans could actually taste regional cuisines from the story's world. The overall effect was a very concrete sense of the world that the show takes place in.

The marketing campaign for *District 9* also did worldbuilding very simply and elegantly, with a series of "Humans Only" ads on bus shelters, benches, and other such places. They took the form of public service announcements instructing the public to call an emergency number if they saw or were exposed to an alien. This little piece of the alien world didn't tell you much about the plot or specific characters of the film, but it did introduce you to the flavor of *District 9*.

Worldbuilding is entry-level transmedia storytelling, and it can be done either for very little money (as in the case of a one-off website complementing an indie film) or for quite a lot of money, as any number of integrated or experiential marketing campaigns will show you.

But seeing how it's been done isn't always helpful in thinking about how you'd do it for your project. So how would you do worldbuilding for *Romeo and Juliet*? For our purposes, think about trying to establish a sense of place and time for Verona, Italy, in the sixteenth century, as a transmedia extension for a performance of the play. Here are my suggestions, just to get your juices flowing.

Depending on the time and resources you have available, you could do any number of things. On the lower end of the budget scale, you could create a website with maps of Verona and the greater region. The design might be heavy in sepia tones, with any writing being either hand-drawn or in a font made to look like it. Extra points if the design looks like a physical atlas, with paper pages.

These maps and the accompanying notes would illustrate the hostility between the Montagues and the Capulets, perhaps by noting the locations of previous brawls or deaths caused by their conflict. It could also foreshadow some of the important locations in the play, such as the apothecary, the church, and even Mantua, the town to which Romeo is banished in the third act.

I'm also personally a big fan of physical artifacts; these would be particularly easy to distribute at a live performance of the play. They can be a very effective means of worldbuilding (although, alas, they can also be very expensive to produce, especially for larger audiences). You could print and distribute invitations to the ball where Romeo and Juliet meet and fall in love, for example. Or perhaps you could

District 9 bus shelter
Courtesy Sony Picture Entertainment

have an illustrated flyer for that apothecary and his services: love potions, sleeping draughts . . . and poisons.

CHARACTERIZATION

Sticking to worldbuilding as the narrative function provides you with room to create some really interesting pieces without worrying too much about whether you're giving away too much of the plot of your story, or dealing with some of the headaches that come along when you start extending characters across media. But if you do have a little more leeway to introduce characters, you can provide an even richer experience.

For marketers, creating characters in the absence of a world or a plot is a strategy that has been used successfully more than once (think of Dos Equis's "Most Interesting Man in the World," or the golden boy of integrated and interactive marketing, Wieden+Kennedy's Old Spice Guy).

So the second compelling artistic purpose for using transmedia tools in your story is to shed light on a character's personality and motivations. This allows the audience to develop knowledge of and connections to your characters in a context that doesn't necessarily need to extend to the action in the main story.

Be forewarned: there are some serious logistical problems to grapple with when you're doing characterization work in an interactive medium as an extension of a static story. It comes down to time and linearity.

Before ∼

A common rookie mistake, especially for projects creating a companion character blog for a film, is to place a character's online presence in an unchanging state. The character is frozen at some point before the story begins, and the blog gives absolutely no information that is relevant to the big-picture narrative. In theory, this might seem to be a good idea—after all, you aren't weakening the impact of your story any by giving the plot away—but the result is generally really boring. Much of the interest a character generates comes from how he dynamically changes over time in response to conflict.

You see, a story typically begins at (or very close to) an inciting moment where conflict begins (it's called *in medias res*, or "in the middle of things"). A common piece of writing advice is to begin your story at the latest possible moment. That moment when the story kicks off is, as it happens, also the moment when your characters become most interesting. If there is no tension because you don't yet have a conflict under way, then your online characters run the risk of being boring, and this might create the false impression that the main story, too, is boring.

So if you create characterization pieces that are frozen in time before your story begins, you have to make sure they are interesting in their own right—something that the audience would enjoy even if they had no knowledge of the other pieces. If your main story is about the hilarious lengths a stamp collector goes to in order to acquire a particularly rare piece of postage, then his online presence should be about how he longs for that stamp, about philately as a whole, or about why he loves stamps.

It shouldn't be about what he had for dinner, the fight he had with his partner over yard work, or how he's been sorting through his junk mail and discovered he hasn't paid the newspaper bill for last month. You could make an argument that all of these things give you a better idea of Mr. Stamp Collector as a character and as a person, but none of that is relevant to the story you're planning on telling with him.

During and After

Positioning your characters after the static piece of the story has concluded can also be problematic—unless you're certain that the audience will see the transmedia extension only after seeing the story, you risk giving away the ending and removing much of the tension from the main event. There is an exception for full-blown, natively transmedia narratives, but let's wait on that for a moment.

And what about doing your characterization work from a point (or from multiple points) during your story? It's a great trick, and there are two ways to do it. The

first is to have your character evolve over time, from the beginning of your story to the end.

Television has a huge advantage over other media in this respect, because of its episodic nature. Any transmedia extension of a character can evolve over time in conjunction with the episodes' air dates. The TV show *How I Met Your Mother* is an absolute pro at creating characterization extensions for a character—in particular, ladies' man Barney Stinson, as played by Neil Patrick Harris. Barney doesn't just have a Twitter feed (@Broslife) sending out pithy commentary for the man who wants to be a player: "Happy Cinco De Mayo . . . or as I call it . . . the day I attempt to score with five chicks from five different Latin countries in one night." He also has his own series of how-to books describing how to live life the way he does, including *The Bro Code*; *The Playbook: Suit up. Score Chicks. Be Awesome*; and *Bro on the Go*.

None of these characterization pieces ties solidly into the overarching storyline of the show, and so by some definitions you could consider them not transmedia at all. But they are nonetheless an extension of the story world that serves a narrative purpose: illuminating the character and philosophy of Barney Stinson, bro extraordinaire.

How I Met Your Mother is by no means alone in using the transmedia toolbox to extend characters, though most TV shows keep it to the web. The Syfy show *Eureka* has a Twitter account for _S_A_R_A_H_, the self-aware computer house on the show, in which she comments on life as a computerized house, talks about her romance with robot-deputy Andy, and foreshadows events that will occur in the next episode to air. The cable network USA, on the other hand, has embraced the method of creating blogs as written by the shows' characters—*Monk*, *Psych*, *Covert Affairs*.

You can also do characterization and a little worldbuilding at the same time. Pam Beesly and Jim Halpert from the show *The Office* had a wedding website (just like a real couple might in the run-up to any real-life marriage), including information on where the wedding would be held and what other activities guests in town might enjoy. After the wedding episode aired, the website was updated to incorporate a gallery of wedding pictures.

Iconic States ⁓

In our example case of *Romeo and Juliet*, the big question is this: when in the story does their online presence exist? Before the play begins, the two of them haven't even met, so their core drama simply doesn't exist. Thus, any extension that occurs before the events of the play would be fundamentally disconnected from what comes after, to such an extent that they might as well be different people once the play begins.

After the play is over, they're both dead. You could extend their characters into the afterlife, or have them as ghosts, but again, this would be fundamentally disconnected from the events and tone of the play itself.

So just how would you build a transmedia extension to characterize Romeo and Juliet?

My solution would be to create something like a Twitter feed, with the pair perpetually frozen in a single, iconic state from the middle of the play. And after a moment's thought, that perpetual state is dead obvious: it has to be after they've met, but before they've married. Think of them as eternally existing in the few hours after the famous balcony scene, always pining for each other, but not yet ready to act on their love.

Some kinds of fiction (James Bond springs to mind) already exist in something close to a single iconic state, making all of this a moot point. And the iconic state is very much a great plan for marketing campaigns that want to create the feeling of a personal relationship with a character, but don't want to play out an actual plot.

We have a stunning example of an iconic, unchanging character in the absence of a plot for consumer marketing: the Old Spice Guy. When actor Isaiah Mustafa wraps that towel around his waist, he becomes a timeless entity representing the tongue-in-cheek appeal of any man who wears Old Spice: a hypothetical perfect man. The extensions of that campaign beyond mere TV commercials have included a Twitter feed and an event where the actor recorded responses to queries on that tweet stream and posted them on YouTube in real time. Those videos have received

millions of views—people seeking out the content to consume because of its entertainment value to them.

If you wanted to take Romeo and Juliet off the web, you could create a volume of letters establishing the relationships between various characters—an unsent letter the Nurse wrote to Juliet, for example, explaining how Juliet took the place of the Nurse's own dead child in her heart, or even angry letters from Lords Montague and Capulet to the Prince of Verona, airing various petty grievances and establishing their enmity.

Stay tuned for more specific tips on how to do characterization in transmedia in a later chapter.

BACKSTORY AND EXPOSITION

Stepping up your game just a little bit more, you can also use a transmedia extension for telling pieces of the story that don't fit into your main narrative, or that shed more and deeper light on the events that happen in your story.

This is where the big fun gets started, and where the line into "definitely transmedia" gets a lot less blurry.

If you stop to think about it, we ask an awful lot from our single-medium stories. They have to carry the entire payload all alone—introduce you to the characters, explain any necessary context and history, and, of course, convey the plot itself. But breaking up your story to put in that context can feel intrusive, especially if it's handled badly.

Think of stopping your action in the middle of an exciting chase sequence because you suddenly have to explain, say, the mechanics of an embezzlement scheme. And then there's the classic: a villain pausing in the middle of murdering the hero in order to deliver a monologue about his plan to conquer the world. That's bad exposition. If it's timed poorly or done to excess, it can completely ruin the pace of your story.

And then again, in the process of creation, you sometimes wind up with a lot of story material that you love, and that would immeasurably enrich or explain the events of your film, TV show, web series, comic, or book, but that you can't work in gracefully because that plot thread about the childhood friend or the lost notebook just doesn't fit. It's too long, too disjointed, or too confusing for a single work.

This is the reason we wind up with director's cuts of a film, DVD extras of omitted scenes, companion atlases, and even the occasional novel featuring the same story, but this time from the point of view of a different character. It's because the creator had too much story to fit into her original work and didn't want to waste all that creative energy.

Maybe you had a romantic subplot that you cut because it made everything too long. Maybe you had to gloss over a rich explanation of the beliefs and origins of a fringe religion in your fiction, because there was no way to incorporate it that wouldn't have come off like inserting an encyclopedia article or infomercial into the plot, bringing all the action and tension to a crashing halt. Maybe there were some well-developed characters whom you simply adored, but who hardly got a walk-on and two lines in the final work.

Good news: there is no longer any reason for compelling material to vanish forever onto the cutting-room floor, or to disappear in edits, just because it made the work too long or you couldn't find a place to fit it into the flow of the story. Explain, expand, and extend by using that bonus material.

Even if you don't have extra material already lying around, there is often still a role for transmedia in smoothing transitions between films, shows, and books (or any combination thereof). There's still a role for using transmedia tools to explain how and why your world works the way it does.

This is an area of transmedia that has not yet been fully tapped, in my opinion: that space between creating one or two transmedia elements for a single-medium work and making a full-blown and completely interactive experience. Such hybrid creations could create a lot of value for both audiences and creators, though, and I fully expect to see more work along these lines in the coming years.

In the Canadian show *The Drunk and On Drugs Happy Funtime Hour*, the online component created by Stitch Media actually covers events that happen between the episodes, and provides significant exposition that fills in the gaps between the episodes of the main show.

In our example case of *Romeo and Juliet*, there is at least one really fascinating untold story boiling under the surface: the origin of the feud between Capulet and Montague. How did it begin? Who is the guiltier party? What was at stake to make the feud so very bloody? There's an entire parallel story just waiting to be fleshed out.

One could do it by creating a complementary graphic novel focused on that origin story: Montague vs. Capulet. Or, if you'd prefer to keep the story closer in tone and feeling to the play itself, you could compose an epistolary drama. Publish the letters that the Montagues and the Capulets wrote to each other, to friends, or to the Prince of Verona—but this time, instead of merely establishing relationships, create a whole separate storyline with its own conflict and resolution—perhaps the story of the Capulets' dire financial situation, meant to explain why they are in such a hurry to marry off their daughter.

Alternatively, you could expand on the crime and punishment elements of the play by creating a game in which the players must take part in a similar family feud. A player would earn points and status for taking action against his hated rival. But he must be careful not to go over the line, or he risks being banished or hanged. Such a game would introduce a player to the dynamics and consequences of such a feud, and thereby make the events in the play easier to understand and relate to.

Once you give yourself permission to find new stories around the edges of your existing story, you won't be able to stop. Where a story ends and where it begins are completely arbitrary, after all; there's always something else that happened before, and something else that will happen after.

NATIVE TRANSMEDIA

Finally, if one is searching for an artistic and narrative function for using transmedia storytelling, there is the ultimate purpose: creating a work that is meant to be entirely and natively transmedia from start to finish, and not a single-medium work at all—an experience that you give to your audience, not just a story you are telling them.

In this scenario, you aren't creating supplemental pieces for a performance, film, or written work. Instead, you're creating a story that is fractured into pieces and conveyed through multiple media, often as though the events were really occurring. The project may sometimes have major single-media components, but they won't give you the whole story on their own.

This is master-class, advanced-level transmedia storytelling. It is complex, chaotic, and performative—and if you do a good job, deeply satisfying for both the audience and the creator.

Entertainment marketing has found great success in playing out an interactive prequel to the main revenue-bearing piece, as evidenced by the many prequel ARGs. In this sort of project, the interactive component ends one moment, and the film begins the very next. But entertainment marketing is really just the tip of the iceberg.

Consumer goods marketing, too, walks this path with great success. The *Mission Icefly* game promoting Wrigley's 5 gum even took the transmedia experience to the next level, incorporating key pieces of content into the packaging of packs of gum, so that the audience needed to purchase the product to continue the story. That's a model we're going to see a lot more of, going forward.

The indie film and experience *Pandemic* is a prime example of a work that was meant to be natively transmedia from start to finish. Director Lance Weiler's ultimate execution included the short film, a live scavenger hunt, and an incredible technology build, plus comics, tweet streams, and more.

At the other end of the spectrum, World Wrestling Entertainment (WWE) is a picture-perfect case study in transmedia storytelling as an ongoing business. WWE puts on live events, of course—the wrestling matches. It also leverages its cross-media capabilities, airing those matches on TV and uploading some of the content to video-sharing sites. The magic, though, comes from WWE's characters extending outside of the ring, with Twitter accounts in persona, where rivalries continue to play out and heat up. WWE wrestlers even appear in character on other shows (*Saturday Night Live*, for example).

Best of all, the WWE keeps a close eye on fan reaction and adapts its storylines to accommodate what the audience loves, what they want more of, and what they completely hate.

If you want to make *Romeo and Juliet* an interactive transmedia experience, the tricky part would be creating a way for the audience to have relationships with the characters. *Romeo and Juliet* as written by Shakespeare doesn't exactly have a clear place for audience participation.

To solve this, I would personally give the audience the part of one of the characters in the story. Not Romeo or Juliet, to be sure, but someone who knows what's going on and takes action to further the story at multiple points in the narrative. Looking with that lens, the right character snaps into focus very quickly: the audience could be Juliet's Nurse.

The Nurse is only a minor character in the play, and yet she has tremendous influence on the outcome of the story. She is the one who arranges the star-crossed lovers' secret marriage, after all. The audience would play the part as Juliet's caretaker, confidante, and advisor. This opens up a dynamic emotional journey for the audience, especially because toward the end of the play, Juliet ceases to confide in the Nurse. Instead, she takes action on her own to secure Romeo's return from Mantua and sets the stage for both of their deaths.

Think about the implications: with the audience as the Nurse, the audience doesn't just feel abstractly sad about the tragedy once the play is over. Instead, they feel both implicitly guilty for their role in bringing the tragedy about, and betrayed by Juliet, who didn't confide in the Nurse in order to get help. The audience would feel that they should have been able to prevent the tragedy, where instead they only ushered it toward its ultimate and unhappy conclusion.

But exactly how do you perform that magic trick? That, dear readers, is what the rest of this book is about.

6 Learn the Basics of Traditional Storytelling

*I*t's possible that you don't come from a storytelling background. Sure, you might already be a filmmaker just looking to expand your film's universe. Or maybe you're a novelist. If that's the case, then you already speak the language of conflict fluently, you know what characterization is, you can draw a nice diagram of good pacing, and you know the relationships between your characters better than you know your own family.

But it's just as likely that you haven't had any formal training or background in storytelling. You might be a marketer, an art director, or a strategist who until now has focused on search engine optimization and microsites. If you don't understand storytelling, then being the best producer or content strategist in the world isn't going to help your transmedia project to be a success.

You can get pretty far on instinct (we're all rampant consumers of stories in this world, and you learn quite a lot just by exposure), but

it's far better to be able to make your creative decisions consciously. With that in mind, let's review some of the bare-bones basics of telling a good story.

CHARACTER

Every story starts with a character. Ideally, your characters will be interesting people, or at least in interesting situations. They don't necessarily have to be people that the audience can relate to or like; they just have to be people that the audience wants to know more about, either because they want to know what happens next or because they want to understand your characters a little better.

But how do you come up with characters like that? Sometimes one will spring into your head, fully formed. This is fantastic when it happens. Unfortunately, though, many of us have to work at it.

One common approach is to reach for the familiar. We model characters on people we know, or on the creations of other writers that we happen to really love. Or sometimes we borrow characters we've seen, not just in one place, but in dozens of places: the authoritarian principal from dozens of movies set in a high school; the grizzled space marine from dozens of video games; the high-born lady with a taste for adventure in dozens (or hundreds, or thousands!) of romance novels.

It's really easy to fall back on these stock characters when we're first building a narrative, especially when we're using bite-sized platforms, where every precious line or second of footage has to carry a tremendous payload of story. These stock characters are a sort of shorthand between you and the audience. Demonstrating what kind of person your character is from scratch takes a lot of time and work, after all. You may be tempted not to bother when you can simply cast a dour-faced man as your principal, put him in a rumpled gray suit, and call it a day.

But it's important that you try to resist the urge to populate your story entirely with these comfortably familiar archetypes. At best, doing so lets you concentrate on the other elements of your story—an understandable goal. At the same time, these shallow characters will limit how invested your audience can be in them; they might feel tired, trite, or boring. Even worse, if you're careless with your stock characters, you might be buying into or perpetuating offensive stereotypes—the sassy gay friend, for example, or the angry black woman.

So if you want to start your character creation process with one of those familiar templates, I highly recommend adding in some character traits that go against the expected type. Take your high school jock and give him a disabled sibling to care for. Give your brassy waitress a happy marriage.

This immediately provides a richness to your characters that makes them a little more multifaceted and resonant. And it gives them a more complex—even unexpected—set of motivations. Bear in mind that your story comes to life in the place where characters and motivations come into contact with a situation.

Once you have your characters, think about what they really want out of life, and what they don't want. What gets them through the day? What drives them to do the things they do? If they won the lottery, what would they do with the money—or is money irrelevant to them? Who or what do they hate more than anything, and why?

Do they have any secrets it would kill them to have discovered—embarrassing, criminal, or sentimental? What are they most afraid of, and why?

You also need to consider how each of your characters feels about the other characters in your story (at least, you do if they'll ever meet). Do they get along? Why or why not? How would you characterize their relationship? How long have they known each other, and how did they first meet? Do they want the same things? Could they work together, if they had to?

CONFLICT

OK, so you have your characters? Great. Now you need to put them into a situation of conflict. Conflict is the beating heart that brings your story to life—the engine that makes your story go. But conflict doesn't necessarily mean fistfights.

Classic narrative theory (as explained by Sir Arthur Thomas Quiller-Couch) has defined only seven basic kinds of conflict that every story is about: man vs. man,

WHY ROMEO AND JULIET?

For many of my examples in this chapter, I keep going back to the classic Shakespeare play *Romeo and Juliet*. Here's why:

1. Most people are already familiar with the rough shape of the story. In the unlikely event that you're not, it's the ultimate romantic tragedy: boy and girl fall in love, but they can never be together because their families detest one another. An unfortunate mix-up ultimately leads to them both committing suicide rather than live without each other. Happy, huh? Wikipedia and *CliffsNotes* can fill you in on more details as you need them.

2. It's public domain, so I'm not stepping on anyone's copyright toes. There's not enough space for a complete primer in this book, but know that there are issues of copyright and credit that you should be very familiar with if you do any work in media today.

3. It's widely regarded as a meaningful cultural work, and it's very different from the kind of fare that's usually seen getting the transmedia treatment. Most high-profile transmedia properties today fall squarely into the science fiction and action/adventure pigeonholes: *A.I.*, *Star Wars*, *Star Trek*, *The Matrix*, *The Dark Knight*, *Halo*, *Lost*. But there really isn't a good reason for that, beyond the fact that those are the kinds of stories that early transmedia creators have themselves been fans of.

   Unfortunately, this has led to a false perception that transmedia is really only good for stories with a heavy mystery or science fiction element. Nothing could be further from the truth. Just because the only thing you've ever used your blender for is to make kale smoothies doesn't mean that it couldn't make a nice piña colada, too. It's time we have more variety in the kinds of stories we tell with transmedia techniques.

man vs. himself, man vs. nature, man vs. society, man vs. supernatural, man vs. machine, and man vs. destiny.

The common thread here is that a character is placed in a position in which she wants something that she can't easily have. A great way to come up with a conflict, then (unless one is already baked into your initial inspiration), is to think very hard about your characters and what their utmost hearts' desires might be. You should already have some idea about this, from when you were thinking about motivations. Is it true love? A promotion? Just living a normal, happy life instead of being press-ganged into a role as the chosen one? Saving the family farm from foreclosure? Coming home safely from the war?

Dangle that possibility in front of their noses, and then come up with a situation in which they can't have it. What do they do?

That's where your story starts.

PLOT

Your plot is what happens to your characters as a result of your conflict. You can think of your plot as a sort of Rube Goldberg machine, where each event leads into the next, and on to the next, with a certain inevitability once the conflict has been established.

Some writers will plan their plot meticulously in advance in an outline or treatment. Others sit down to the page and just go, and find out what happens next as it flows out of their subconscious. Neither method is superior, but you have to absolutely and without question understand what work each part of your story is doing.

It is especially important in transmedia to have a plot that goes from beginning to end before you launch. It's fine for that plot to be a skeleton with little to no meat on it, but you have to know where you're going, or you risk your story meandering, bogging down, or fizzling out entirely somewhere in the middle. There are few things worse than realizing that you've painted yourself into a corner in front of a live audience, so to speak.

In this initial plotting, you may find that your starting idea just isn't strong enough to carry the story the whole way. If you get stuck on what happens next, one good trick is to introduce a new element that throws a wrench into your story's status quo—a car crash or other accident, a freak storm, an election, even a whole new character entering the scene. Play with each idea for a while, and think through the implications the way you might with a game of chess. Stay a few moves ahead. If it still isn't working, go back a few steps and change something.

Every house has what are called load-bearing walls; those are the support beams that hold up the roof, and if you were to knock down those walls, the house would fall down, too. Likewise, every story has what I call load-bearing plot points—those pivotal moments that absolutely have to occur if the rest of the story is to hold together coherently. Often these are changes in your characters' relationships and motivations over the course of the story.

In *Romeo and Juliet*, it isn't particularly crucial for Romeo and his friends to make fun of the Nurse, as they do in one scene, but if the tragic pair don't meet and fall in love, then nothing else in the play makes sense. That's a load-bearing plot point. In *Star Wars*, you need Luke to receive near-death visions of Obi-Wan Kenobi to understand why he goes to the planet Dagobah to be trained by Yoda; you could remove that particular element, but if you did, you'd have to replace it with something else that does the same job of motivating Luke to abandon his post and find Yoda.

As you become comfortable with plotting, you'll begin to discover that the specifics of the plot are practically irrelevant. The important thing is the web of tensions and relationships that occur as a result of each piece. If you need a character to be in a bad mood, it might be because the milk for her morning coffee went sour, or because she got into a car accident on the way to work, or because she's received a notice that the Wizard's Union will be auditing her reagents inventory.

However, if the piece you use to do that work is too showy, then it might overshadow the main part of your story. That car accident on the way to work has a cascade of implications involving health, stress levels, money, and time—if you just need your character to be in a bad mood for one morning (and not bogged down in insurance claims for the next week), then the accident might not be your best choice to put her in that mood.

Plot is very much like a complicated machine. If you want to be able to tinker with it and not have it break, you need to figure out how it works in the first place. The only way to do that, though, is trial and error. Your instincts will get better, and you'll err less over time.

RISING TENSION

We all want to make our stories really gripping, the kind of thing that people can't stop reading or watching, and can't stop thinking about between installments. A lot goes into making that happen, but one of the most important elements is rising tension.

Through the course of the story, you need to provide the feeling that things are getting worse and worse. More and more must be at stake all the way up until the end, when all or most of the tension is resolved (for better or for worse).

It's especially easy to see the stakes gradually but steadily raised in comics or action movies, but rising tension is used everywhere, even in classic literature. Romeo and Juliet fall in love, and their families hate each other. That's pretty bad. Then they secretly marry, so there's suddenly more at stake than the two pining for one another across a balcony rail; they've made a vow. Then Romeo kills Juliet's cousin and is banished to another city, leaving Juliet a secret but abandoned wife who must choose whether to honor her marriage vow and betray her family's hopes for her, or abandon true love but get along with her family. The situation gets steadily more awful for them without stop until the story's tragic conclusion.

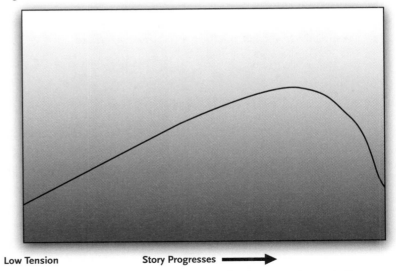

Tension rises from the beginning to the end of a story

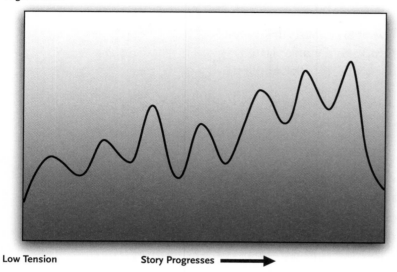

High Tension

Low Tension   Story Progresses ━━━━▶

Tension should rise and fall, but the general trend is upward

That's not to say that there should be no respite for your characters, or that nothing good should ever happen to them. Ideally, they should be subjected to a series of ups and downs, as long as the general trend is toward more tension, higher stakes, and worse situations—at least up until your climax, when your tension needs to resolve enough to leave the audience satisfied. Really, the emotional arc of your story should look something more like it does in the chart to the left.

There is quite a lot of narrative theory one could apply here. If you're responsible for the overall shape of your story, it's a good plan to learn more about the formal three-act structure, the five-act structure, and Joseph Campbell's thoughts on the classic hero's journey. You can certainly experiment with other forms, but it's always a better idea to experiment only once you have a solid grounding in what has and hasn't worked in the past, and why.

SETTING AND MOOD

Once you have the skeleton of your story providing its general shape, you can move toward filling in detail and deciding whether it will have feathers or fur, so to speak. You'll need to start making choices about setting, mood, and even theme. It's best if you make these creative decisions in parallel with big-picture structural questions about which media to use and how to guide your audience from one to the next.

Setting is of paramount importance in transmedia storytelling. Your setting is where your story takes place—the world your characters inhabit. Often it's the same world as ours (or at least a small cross section of it), plus or minus a few fictional characters. One of the things transmedia excels at is worldbuilding—that is, establishing the feeling that your fictional place really exists, or showing what it's like even beyond the scope of the characters on stage.

Mood, on the other hand, is the general tone of your story: lighthearted or serious, sarcastic or somber. Mood will be reflected in what occurs in your plot, but also in how it's presented: the lighting for video and photography, the specific words used in text, even the colors and fonts of a website. Ultimately, mood is the cumulative result of a thousand small creative decisions over the span of a project.

Setting and mood can be more difficult to manage for a transmedia narrative than for single-medium stories, because each component may have a different creative team behind it. If that's the case, then you need to have some baseline understanding shared among all of your creative teams of what your story should look and feel like, for the sake of continuity. A story about heroic adventures in the Amazon shouldn't take a left turn and become a comedy of manners when it switches to another medium.

That definitely doesn't mean that you need the same plots to repeat themselves endlessly, and you don't need to always convey the same moral messages. But you do at least need to maintain a baseline consistency of tone.

If you absolutely must break consistency by having one element be comical and another dead serious, be sure you're doing it for a purpose. A business goal might be tapping multiple markets—for example, bringing an adult-focused story to the children's market. An artistic goal could be establishing an unreliable narrator. Just be cautious; changing tones is not a technique to be used lightly.

THEME

Somewhere deep inside, your story is about something more than your characters and your plot. And I don't mean on the surface level, where your story is about (say) a boy and a girl falling in love; it's the message that's dressed up in your plot. For Romeo and Juliet, you could say that the theme is one of hatred destroying everything. (Though, to be fair, Shakespeare was a very rich writer, and it's difficult to pin

The First Folio, a 1623 collection of Shakespeare's plays

him to just one theme. You could just as easily say that our favorite play is about the lengths people will go to for love, even when it goes against their own best interests.)

Ideally, you know what your story is about at its heart. But I consider consciously writing with a theme in mind to be an advanced technique. It's more my style to write a work, then discover when I'm nearly done that it's about something that I didn't notice or realize when I was in the thick of it. My first (unpublished and honestly pretty awful) novel was on the face of it a story about a woman in Fairyland. But once I finished, I realized that it was all about how complicated the relationships between mothers and children can be (very deeply so)—perhaps not surprising considering that I was expecting my first child when I wrote it.

So don't feel bad if you decide to ignore theme for now. Just know that it's in there, and look around for it as you go. Once you find it, you may see opportunities to tweak the details of your story here and there to resonate more strongly with that theme.

ORIGINALITY

It's easy to think that your story needs to be incredibly original to be good, and that if you have a great idea, that's enough to pull the audience through the whole thing. Nothing could be further from the truth.

There are entire industries built around telling the same basic stories again and again. The entire romance novel industry, for example, thrives on endless permutations of the same story: two people falling in love and overcoming obstacles to live happily ever after. Another common story is the one in which a crime is committed, and a detective (or someone acting as a detective) must find and collar the culprit.

But these stories and others remain evergreen because of window dressing and details of execution. You could sit two writers down and tell them exactly what story to write, but their stories would always be completely different.

FURTHER RESEARCH

This has been just a light once-over on the basics of good storytelling—enough to get you through this book, but probably not enough to build a rockin' career with no further outside wisdom. If you're a creator who doesn't have a strong storytelling background already, I highly recommend that you read these books, for a start:

On Writing, Stephen King   *Writing the Breakout Novel*, Donald Maass

Story, Robert McKee   *Writing Down the Bones*, Natalie Goldberg

You can also gain a lot from joining a writer's group or an established online community. Giving and receiving critiques from other writers can help you to identify your strengths and weaknesses as a creator. Talking with other writers about writing can help you learn about what works for other people, too. It might not always work for you, because everyone's work and creative processes are different, but more knowledge is never a bad thing.

And if you're serious about becoming better at telling stories, it is of the utmost importance that you look at all the movies you watch, the books you read, and the games you play with a critical eye. Analyze the characters and what their motivations are; map out in your head the patterns of rising and falling tension. See if you can spot underlying themes. Try to take the story apart in your head like a watch; and once you've broken it into its component pieces, try to put it back together again so you understand exactly how it works.

But most of all, keep writing, and then do the same thing to your own stories. Be brutal with yourself about what does and doesn't work. The conventional wisdom is that you have to write a million words of garbage before you get to the good stuff. It takes even longer (and maybe never happens at all) if you aren't looking at your work with a hard, critical eye toward improvement.

If you keep working at it, you will inevitably get better and better. Don't ever give up. Just keep working at telling better stories.

All that said, if you have an idea for a story that you think is really crazy, and you genuinely think nobody has done anything like it before, don't let that get in your way, either. Make the stories that speak to you, whatever they are.

Q&A: NAOMI ALDERMAN

Naomi Alderman is the award-winning author of the novels *Disobedience*, *The Lessons*, and *The Liar's Gospel*. She was also the lead writer on *Perplex City* and the runaway crowdfunding success *Zombies, Run!*, a mobile, story-driven running game.

Q: *Where do you see the art and business of storytelling headed over the next few years?*

A: Well, I don't think we're going to lose our taste for stories, that's for sure. We're surrounded by more and more stories, and not just in drama: in reality TV, in advertising, on product packaging, not to mention in our conversations. Sometimes I feel that every different part of our lives is somehow being turned into a story. And the traditional linear story will always have a place.

But we're interacting with each other differently, too. We expect to receive messages from our friends on the fly everywhere we go, so stories are likely to follow us there as well. And stories are becoming more complex. If you compare something like *The Wire* with *Leave It to Beaver*, there's a huge complexity multiplier, not just in the moral world, but also in character depth, number of stories happening at any point, and number of characters you're expected to keep track of. We're getting better at keeping up with more complex stories, so I expect that trend to just keep going, or even accelerate.

Q: *What would you recommend that transmedia creators learn about to improve their craft?*

A: Role-playing games are the best possible training, I think, for writing and running a story on the fly. I especially love *Call of Cthulhu*. Read *Masquerade*, if you haven't before, and see how it's put together: pictures and words that tell a story together, but more than a story, a whole experience. You could do worse than take an improv class! And make something: something small, maybe just for your friends. You'll learn more by making a small experience and seeing what works and what doesn't than by taking a dozen classes.

Q: *How is transmedia storytelling different from writing flat novels—and how is it the same?*

A: Certain things remain the same: a good character is the same. Good characters are complex and multilayered, which means that they want more than one thing, feel two different emotions about the same person, sometimes contradict themselves, have secrets and fears. Good people are sometimes bad. Bad people can sometimes be good.

And the question of *why* you're telling this story remains the same, I think. Even if you're advertising a product, even if you're working for someone else, you need to find somewhere that the story connects with *you*—with what you believe, with what you've experienced, with your own truth. I think that if you don't believe it, you won't be able to tell it.

And now how is it different? Well, primarily, I think, because you need to leave room for your players or your audience. You give up a little bit of control, in exchange for input from your audience that can absolutely bring a story to life. The difference is basically in the arena of plot: you get to make the characters, you get to decide what the story's about, but you don't get to decide every element of the plot, because wonderful, unpredictable human beings are in there.

Q: *What does it take to get good at telling stories?*

A: The same thing as it takes to get to Carnegie Hall: practice, practice, practice. Keep writing. Finish things. You will never ever ever ever ever get better if you leave everything half finished, or keep on revising the first bit over and over.

Push through, even if you know it's terrible. Only when you've finished it will you know what you have, and will you be able to learn how to do it better next time.

Some things I had to learn: pacing, and how to trust myself. Early on I had a lot of problems with getting so excited that I could actually finish a story that I, um, ended prematurely. It's good to concentrate on . . . how to draw it out for long enough to make it enjoyable without going on so long that the reader gets completely exhausted. Luckily, with writing, you can put your story away for a few weeks and then experience it very fresh when you pick it up again.

And on trusting myself: the longer you go on, the more you know that a story will just emerge if you let it. If you follow your thought, if you don't squash it and say, "Oh, I can't tell *that* truth, I can't talk about *that* part of life." I can highly recommend an exercise I did once for a project I was working on: writing a full story every day for 21 days. After that, I saw that sometimes what emerged was terrible, sometimes it was great, but just putting in the work was what was important.

7

How Story and Branding Affect Marketing

You *may be asking yourself, does story really have to have all this stuff? Themes and* moods and rising tension? What if I'm in marketing—it doesn't apply to me then, does it?

Folks in the advertising business often refer to themselves as storytellers, but this can cause some eye rolling when it comes up in other circles. That's because the ad industry uses the word *story* a little differently from the way novelists, playwrights, and filmmakers do. In entertainment, it's generally agreed that a story has certain key characteristics: characters, a plot, cause and effect. Marketers, though, often use the word *story* to mean something subtly different; it refers to a message, imagery intended to evoke a specific idea or emotional response, a web of quickly understood tensions and dynamics.

This is a little more defensible than those of us on the story-equals-plot side of the argument might like to admit. After all, there is the classic six-word short "story" allegedly by Ernest Hemingway:

For sale. Baby shoes. Never worn.

Like an ad, that doesn't explicitly give you characters or a plot—or does it? On a little reflection, you'll realize there are some invisible characters that aren't spelled out in the text of the story. A sale necessitates the existence of a seller, after all, and the kind of people who would be selling unused baby shoes are the kind who desperately want a baby but don't have one. Those six words can evoke a scenario of parents grieving over an infant's too-small coffin with terrible ease. (There are other stories one could read into it, too—one of a desperately wanted child who has never been conceived, for example.) Likewise, any number of ads and marketing campaigns can be perceived as ultra-condensed stories, with significant elements only implied and unspoken.

In this book, I'm mostly addressing the basic structure of story as seen through a novelist's or screenwriter's eyes, because this is infinitely relevant to today's full-blown, narrative-based marketing campaigns. But the marketer's point of view is still important, and the tools marketers use are helpful for a transmedia storyteller to learn (even outside of marketing).

The ability to conjure up a web of tensions and an emotional response with just a photo and a few words, or with 30 seconds of video? That's a skill you can put to work. It requires you to develop a keen eye for what the most important and emotive moments are in the story you're telling, and to pare away anything extraneous until only the most distilled essence of it remains. Knowing intimately where the true heart of your story lies (and, by extension, what inspires people to care about it) is important to any storyteller, in any industry, in any medium.

There are a few concerns and caveats specific to using transmedia storytelling for branding purposes, though. Let's address those now.

NO BRANDCUFFS

Let's say you're building a transmedia marketing campaign for some sort of consumer commodity—bar soap, for example. It's a marketer's natural instinct to look at everything through the lens of promoting the product. You might start with the proposition that your story has to be about soap, and that it has to feature people who are really excited about soap in new scents, with new stain-fighting powers, or whatever other miraculous soap innovation is making it to store shelves next.

This is a really, really bad idea.

You hear engagement bandied about as one of the advantages of social media in general and transmedia in particular. In a general sense, building engagement means making people actually care about what it is that you're making. At its most basic level, engagement means that people want to know what happens next, or what's happened so far. They want more of your story.

Sounds obvious, right? To get your audience engaged, you have to make something they're going to care about. But it's sometimes difficult for creators to distance themselves from their work enough to recognize that what the audience cares about isn't necessarily the same thing as what the creator cares about.

In the real world, allegiance to a soap brand isn't something that people care much about. It doesn't come up very often at parties or around the water cooler. It's of crucial importance to people who work for a soap company (or have a soap company as a client), but your soap-centered story isn't going to engage your audience unless there is something more robust under that gentle layer of bubbles. You might make an exception for something campy and tongue-in-cheek, but you certainly can't do it with a straight face.

Television and radio of days gone by got that, and in spades. The original soap operas made sure you knew that soap was the sponsor, but they didn't make sure the actual drama revolved around Joan noticing that her daughter-in-law Ellen had started using an off brand, exposing her beloved son to the horrors of graying shirts. That approach became successful in advertising in the latter half of the twentieth century, but it's increasingly difficult to capture a consumer's time and attention to watch a bald-faced commercial message. And it's only going to get harder from here.

So nowadays, you have to shift your focus. Take off your brand goggles and be mindful of how important your product genuinely is to the average consumer. This can be really hard. But it's an unskippable step if you want your story to have the desired effect.

There's a related issue, too, of how hard to push your brand in the content of the story itself, even if you accept that the brand won't be the star. If you want to use a transmedia story as a branding effort, the traditional mindset would insist that you work your product (or brand) in there somehow. Why spend all of that money building out a transmedia story if nobody ever knows who's behind it?

The answer, of course, is that you can and should make it clear that you're involved, as long as you do it lightly. Truly excellent transmedia marketing has more in common with a Hollywood film than with a commercial—except that it doesn't just entertain, it also shows the audience that your brand cares about the same things they do. The Audi promotional game *Art of the Heist* was about stolen cars, putting the brand front and center, but the narrative wasn't fundamentally about the cars, it was about the characters.

The brand doesn't even need to make an appearance in the story proper. The MTV show *Valemont* was sponsored by Verizon Wireless. To be sure, each episode began and ended with a video clip playing, framed in a Verizon phone, and some pieces of content could be accessed early by using a for-pay service available to Verizon's mobile phone subscribers. This conveyed Verizon's involvement efficiently and promoted its brand, without at any point breaking into commercial speech about Verizon's line of service offerings, which would have disrupted the narrative. It was graceful; the audience knew it was Verizon without having the brand promoted ad nauseam.

But there's also potential for a brand to sponsor entertainment while remaining hands-off regarding the content entirely, as has happened with Xbox Live and

Sprint, both sponsors of the hit web series *The Guild*. It's not a new idea; decades ago, the financial institution Mutual of Omaha sponsored a series of wildlife shows. A generation was thoroughly saturated with those memories of watching *Mutual of Omaha's Wild Kingdom*. The show had nothing to do with insurance or banking, but I'll tell you that even now, 30 years later, I still think of Mutual of Omaha every time I see a nature show. This sponsorship model has fallen into disuse in recent decades, but it's high time for that model of branded entertainment to make a big comeback.

You can even do outright product placement, as with those Audis in *Art of the Heist*; just don't be heavy-handed about it. If the story starts to feel like a hard sell or an infomercial, or if the characters start to come off as brand shills and not as living people with varied motivations, then your story loses its value as entertainment. If it's not entertaining, nobody will seek it out. And transmedia storytelling is, again, all about making something engaging—something that people will care about enough to seek it out.

The lesson here is that even if you're a marketer, you need to consider your audience's experience first and foremost. If you're not providing an experience that your audience is going to value, you're just wasting your client's money. Entertaining is the new marketing.

SO WHERE TO BEGIN?

For traditional entertainment properties like films and TV shows, applying transmedia storytelling techniques in your marketing campaign is fairly easy. You already have a world, and you probably already have some characters; ideally, the creative team for the main show will collaborate on the marketing piece, sharing all of the same assets and resources, if not the same talent.

That's because the experience you can provide when you integrate every single transmedia element is vastly superior. Indeed, thinking of the transmedia components as separate entities at all might be something of a mistake. *Blair Witch*

producer Mike Monello has said that he wouldn't even call the *Blair Witch* transmedia narrative an extended experience because "it was never concepted as 'in addition to' the movie but was always written and created as part of it. Even much of the documentary stuff was originally shot for the original film, which is why it feels so much of a piece rather than a movie with a bunch of extended stuff—it all came from the same place."

As *The Blair Witch Project* demonstrates, the more an entertainment campaign feels like it's all one piece with the movie, show, or novel being marketed, the more successful it will be at engaging and energizing fans.

It gets a little more complicated, though, when the marketing campaign is for a nonentertainment brand. You don't start with all that heavy lifting already done for you. That means you have to give long and serious thought to what kinds of stories are consistent with your brand message. An exciting thriller featuring espionage and black market dealings might be a great choice for an auto manufacturer . . . but maybe not so compatible with the overall image of a supermarket. A soap-style drama about sex and betrayal wouldn't be a great choice for a diaper manufacturer.

Unfortunately, there are no easy-to-apply formulas that can tell you what kind of story is right for any given brand. It might help to think about what values you want to show your audience you care about, or even what adjectives you'd like applied to your brand, and see if you can come up with a story to fit the bill. An athletic shoe company might want something exciting and competitive, like that thriller. A teen hygiene brand might want something youthful and personal, so a story about high school romance could work. A bank trying to convey that it has a strong history but is moving into the future might consider updating a classic story to be set in the present.

At the end of the day, though, only you (or you and your client working together) can decide what your story should be about. What I can help you with, though, is how to tell your story for best effect.

8

Writing for Transmedia Is Different

Writing for any major stand-alone pieces of a transmedia experience is already a well-examined topic. There's no great mystery about how to write for comics, for film, for TV. There are books to buy and classes to take; they're fairly mature forms.

Each of these media comes with its own particular challenges, too. When you're writing a novel, you have to wrestle with tense and point of view. Generally agreed-upon hallmarks of good writing include "show, don't tell" and the rule of Chekhov's gun. If you're writing a screenplay, you need to develop a visual sense for how your scenes and sequences will carry your meaning.

Many of these storytelling techniques for single media still apply in transmedia, but others just don't—and if that isn't confusing enough, there are new considerations that come into play, new tools to use, and some traditional advice you're better off ignoring entirely.

In this and in the next few chapters, we'll be concentrating mainly on the requirements of telling a single, highly fragmented story across multiple platforms, and most particularly across digital platforms—you might call it social media storytelling as much as transmedia. That's because this is where the methods of traditional single-platform or flat narratives become inadequate. Not all of these suggestions will apply to you or to your project, but it's a good idea to be aware of them, just in case.

In the production chapters, I offer more specific tips on how to adapt single pieces of media so that they integrate more easily with a larger transmedia storyline. But for now, let's zoom out and look at the big picture. How is writing for transmedia different from any other kind of writing?

CHEKHOV'S GUN

Chekhov's gun is generally regarded as a brilliant principle for writing tight narrative. The Russian playwright Anton Chekhov wrote: "If in the first act you have hung a pistol on the wall, then in the following one it should be fired." He elaborates that if you don't plan to fire your firearm in a subsequent act, then it doesn't belong in your story, and you should remove it entirely.

The widely accepted interpretation is that nothing should be present in your story unless it's serving some critical narrative purpose. Judicious application of Chekhov's gun can rid your story of elements that aren't doing anything for you.

It might well be that you're better off without that methodical scene in which a character checks into her hotel room, takes a shower, and goes to sleep for the night. And it's true, if you leave too many loose ends floating around, your finale risks leaving the reader feeling dissatisfied. For single-medium narratives, it's an important reminder that you need to be aware of what work each scene, paragraph, and sentence is performing to keep your story rolling along.

There are problems with Chekhov's gun even in traditional media, though, particularly where it meets up with Occam's razor. From time to time, I've found a storyteller adhere so zealously to the gun principle that an entire story unravels into tired predictability. If your story is wound so tightly that every element serves a single, distinct function, the discerning reader can often deduce what that function is. Yawn. So the principle is always best used with a bit of caution.

And once you move into transmedia, you just might be better off forgetting you ever heard Chekhov's name at all.

LOCATE YOUR EXITS

Novelist Jim D. MacDonald gives writing advice on the online forum Absolute Write under the name Uncle Jim. He advocates that everything in a novel should reveal character, advance plot, or support theme. This is advice I can very nearly agree with. For transmedia, I'd add one more item to Uncle Jim's list: adding color to your world.

Part of the juggling act that is telling a transmedia story involves creating depth and richness. To make your world come to life, you need to signal that there are more and deeper stories going on in that world than the single narrative at hand— your world has to seem bigger than your characters. That means introducing elements that provide color and flavor to your transmedia world, even if they won't be immediately relevant to the story you're telling.

But there's another reason to do this in transmedia, too. You need to build in escape routes and back doors, because you never know when you'll need to make a hasty exit. This is particularly the case if you're planning on telling an ongoing or interactive narrative and will be adding to the story as you go. Transmedia storytelling is an exercise in open-ended storytelling, boundless where a traditional single-medium story is finite.

I wrote two years of fictional news articles for the *Perplex City Sentinel*, and in the process, I left so many guns lying about (so to speak) that you'd think a war would break out by the end. Nothing ever came of fast food purveyor Crispy Heaven's

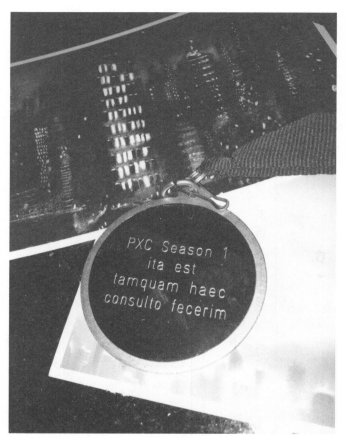

Perplex City's **story team received these medallions after Season 1**

health violations. We never went anywhere with a news short about 78-year-old puzzle design superstar Alan Willow, and the cracks in the seaside Mobius Strip entertainment hub were, indeed, nothing but ordinary wear and tear, never to be spoken of again.

But for every throwaway piece of color that we never touched again, there was another piece that we picked up on our needles and knit into the fabric of the story weeks or months or years later, because suddenly it solved a problem that we hadn't seen coming or added a complication that made for a more interesting story. A mayoral election produced an entire political subplot. A recording mogul became the employer of a sociopathic killer at the heart of the central mystery. A name fabricated as a source for a single quote—Helena Frye—became a double agent working for the police to undermine a secret society.

We never knew what we'd need next, but we knew that we could look back on our established canon and be sure we'd find something that would help us out of our latest pickle. We did this so often that it became our team motto: *Ita est tamquam haec consulto fecerim.* It's Latin for, "It's like we did it on purpose."

Your takeaway: the multithreaded and sometimes reactive nature of transmedia means that you can't always go back and revise your first act to include a gun if it turns out, now that you're in the third act, that you really need one. Sprinkle your story with guns, just in case—leave yourself space to work in. It's a curious opposite to narrative structure in a single-medium story. In transmedia, if you don't leave yourself enough loose ends, the resulting overarching story might actually be weaker.

THE WEIGHT PARADOX

That's not to say that you have carte blanche to leave loose ends floating around hither and thither without a care. If you do it poorly, your audience is going to be dissatisfied with those guns you're leaving sprinkled about, because you can accidentally create narrative expectations that never achieve any kind of payoff.

Each medium has accepted conventions for how to indicate that something is going to be important: size, volume, focus. In a film, if the camera lingers on a shot of an apple for a moment, that's an indicator that the apple is not just scenery; it's important somehow. In a newspaper, the most important stories are toward the front and at the top, with the biggest headlines. In dance or theater, the lead gets a spotlight.

In text-only fiction, if you mention something once, it might just be color. If you go on about it for a paragraph, you're imbuing it with more weight. If you mention it separately a second and even a third time, but then never go anywhere with it by the end, then you're leaving a loose end hanging. Cue audience frustration.

And in transmedia? Examine this from the ARG perspective. This is a form that delights in hiding information in the subtlest, tiniest ways: Mysterious film credits and Morse code in the background of an audio file. Hidden links in source code. Significant clues left out of focus in the background of a photograph, which is only one of many photographs in a Flickr stream.

This presents us with a problem, as creators. In a genre in which absolutely anything might be important, how can you tell the audience when something is not important, and that not only are they barking up the wrong tree, but they've got the wrong forest entirely?

And believe me, it does happen. I've seen it more times than I care to count—audiences latching onto something that was just a design element (the splatter border of a photograph) or an offhand piece of color (a horoscope urging the eating of eel and cucumber rolls) to try to come up with some deeper meaning that sheds light on a narrative element, even where none was ever intended.

In my projects, we are constantly removing elements and references that we worry that our audience will make too much of, since we don't want to lead them down too many dead ends. But there's no predicting what will be taken as an inadvertent clue. It happens anyway, and it's always something we'd thought completely innocuous.

What's a creator to do? I actually don't have a solution for this, beyond what I've been doing in my own work: I try not to make the kind of structure where the border on a photograph might ever be important. When something is important, I try to find ways to make that clear, with weight and design and color and, above all, by saying it with the voices of my characters.

So this is the caveat for abandoning the Chekhov's gun principle. Leave your guns sprinkled around, absolutely. But don't shine a spotlight on any of them until you know which ones you're planning on using.

MULTIPLATFORM PAYOFFS

There's more to writing for transmedia than simply leaving yourself a lot of loose ends that you can pick up later, of course. The Chekhov's gun problem, and the tension between leaving yourself space and not creating expectations you can't fulfill, segues nicely into a new and transmedia-centric variation on his rule. In transmedia, if you have a gun hanging on the wall in the movie, it must be fired in the comic.

This isn't meant to be taken literally, of course, just as Chekhov's original rule is only a guideline. But both of them go toward the same thing: managing expectations. Chekhov wants you to give your audience a payoff by the end of your story for expectations that you establish early on. I want you to create story elements in one medium that have their payoffs in another medium.

It can be a big, interactive piece, like *Why So Serious?*'s collaborative bus theft leading into *The Dark Knight*'s school-bus-as-getaway-car. But it doesn't have to be enormous or plot-shaking. If you know, for example, that Romeo is to be banished to Mantua in the film version, you might make a big deal of showing that he hates Mantua, that he considers it a dull backwater with no nightlife, as part of your world-building efforts. This creates even more tension around the subject of Mantua and heightens the stakes when he is sent there.

It's easiest to do this backward, when you can—know what moments are coming in one element, so that you can build toward them in earlier media. This is much simpler to do if your structure incorporates both long-production components (like film or a video game) and faster-to-produce media, like social media streams or web content.

With a deft touch, you can even turn prosaic or comic moments into a payoff, because you've imbued them with significance where there was none before. If a character fumbles with a coffee cup, drops it, and it breaks in one medium, you can build backward from there so that this is just the latest in a long series of broken cups, turning something that could have just been a symptom of one moment of feeling shaken into the last straw. Or maybe you can build in a history of that particular coffee cup, making it a gift from a beloved but deceased friend to add fresh poignancy to that moment.

The benefit for this is creating that "greater than the sum of its parts" feeling. As a creator, you also gain the ability to create layers upon layers of meaning across your story, which in turn rewards your audience for their engagement. Audience members who have participated in or consumed both parts of your story will feel a deeper connection to the whole.

And that moment when everything comes into focus and they understand how everything fits together—that moment is magic, for you and for them.

9

Online, Everything Is Characterization

Creating compelling characters is one of the most crucial tasks confronting any narrative, in any medium. In a novel or flat-text short story, your tool-set for characterization is pretty well understood: you provide telling details about the characters and their interactions with one another through dialogue, descriptions of body language, and so on. When done well, this allows you to convey a wealth of information about background, outlook, personality—all the things that make characters *who they are*.

In print, I could describe someone as a burly fellow with a neon green Mohawk and a studded leather jacket, and you'd have some idea of what that person was like and where he was coming from. Or in film, I could show you a lady with dainty pearl earrings and a prim dress with a Peter Pan collar, and you'd know that was probably a very different person from Mohawk Dude. These visual clues signal a lot

about the characters and provide context to help you understand why they act the way they do over the course of a story.

But characterization in transmedia shares only a little with characterization in printed text; it has more in common with a comic book or a traditional video game. For transmedia stories, you need to develop a very strong and distinct visual sense, and one that goes beyond just knowing what your characters look like. This is particularly true when you're writing web-based fiction, where you generally don't have the liberty of describing a character with one or two telling details and leaving it at that. You might not even get a graceful moment for description at all, so you have to find other ways to telegraph that information.

The tools you have for characterization across multiple platforms are more varied and demanding than their equivalent in text, too. You must be vigilant about maintaining consistency of character via a hundred tiny visual, technical, and typographical cues. If you plan to include photos or video, you can incorporate description through casting, costuming, and setting, as you would in film. But the ways in which character is revealed in transmedia extend far beyond what people look like and how they move into everything they do—and exactly how they do it.

If Mohawk Dude will be keeping a blog, the design must be one that he would choose as his public face, and it must be in keeping with his personality in terms of color, layout, design, which fonts to use, even whether or not photos have been artificially distressed. You can learn a lot about a character who chooses a hot-pink floral blog theme and uses Comic Sans as the font as compared to a minimalist black-and-white site that sticks to Helvetica.

The same goes for Twitter profile themes and other customizable components of social media. Mohawk Dude and Pearl Earrings probably wouldn't want or like the same design elements. If you're not taking personality into consideration in your design phase, you're missing out on an important tool for characterization.

Don't get too wrapped up in justifying the technology underlying the character's presence, though. I used to make myself crazy considering realism—I worried that the character would have to somehow know how to put up sites and profiles of that complexity to justify their existence. But it's an emerging convention not to overthink personal websites with production values that exceed the plausible skill of the character in question. Audiences don't generally care about it in the first place. So don't let mere realism trip you into weakening your storytelling arsenal.

BEYOND THE VISUAL

Ideally, everything about a character will be internally consistent. Even the media platforms you choose can build character.

A character who primarily uses LinkedIn will be perceived as different from the sort of person who uses Facebook; your LinkedIn user will be considered all business, and it won't be your venue of choice if your story is going to involve intense interpersonal drama. Gmail and AOL email addresses bring up very different connotations—the Gmail user will be considered technology-savvy, the AOL user not so much.

There will be projects where these media choices will be made for structural reasons instead of purely creative ones (or because of a partnership agreement, or because only one choice has a pivotal feature that you need). That means you won't always have the liberty to work them for maximum character-building power. But do examine your platform decisions whenever you have the opportunity; every little touch helps.

And don't forget that one of the best tools for showing character even in flat fiction is still there for you: what the character actually does in your story. All the great visual detail and telling media choices in the world won't help you if your character doesn't do interesting things for interesting reasons. Action speaks to motivation and character like nothing else.

VOICE AND DIALOGUE

Dialogue is a tricky thing, even in flat single-medium storytelling. It needs to sound plausible, but not too realistic. (It turns out that real dialogue is boring to read.)

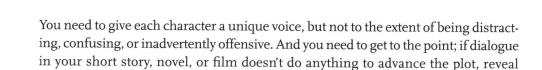

You need to give each character a unique voice, but not to the extent of being distracting, confusing, or inadvertently offensive. And you need to get to the point; if dialogue in your short story, novel, or film doesn't do anything to advance the plot, reveal character, or support your theme, the odds are good that you don't need it at all.

These are structural concerns with dialogue—the things that will affect the content of your story. There are also creative concerns, though, regarding how to string the actual words together to sound like the character who is speaking. The sound and pattern of the words chosen is called *voice*.

Voice is important in writing dialogue for flat fiction, but it's about a hundred times more important in social media storytelling. In transmedia, everything you write for a character is, essentially, dialogue. Sometimes this is literally true, as in the lines for a video script, but sometimes it's true more figuratively. A blog post, for example, should be written in the style your character uses to write—not yours. These are words that your character has directly chosen, and they should reflect her personality.

Think about all the potential elements of a project that can wind up as written words: blog posts, tweets, photo captions, emails, status updates, letters, or postcards. Then there are the spoken words in phone calls, voice mail messages, video clips, and so on. Every word of this is dialogue, in a sense. Ideally, every scrap of it will reveal and support character.

Accordingly, you need to hone your character's writing voice and make it distinct, not just with regard to where it appears and what it says, but with how it reads. Does a character say "dude" all the time? Drop subjects? Does he use contractions? Swear a lot, or never? Capitalize Random Words? Overuse emoticons and punctuation!?!? :D :D. What kind of emoticons? :-) B`} ∧_∧ Does she use l33t sp34k or txt abbrvtns? Does he insert action descriptors *types furiously* to show you what he's doing or thinking?

Know how your character writes and stick to it. Waffling between different methods, unless you do it for a specific effect (like dropping emoticons when a character gets serious) is going to muddle up your characterization. That hurts your story.

The omnipresence of dialogue has some more far-reaching implications for transmedia storytelling, too. Every piece of content you put out there from a character says something about who that character is—and about who she wants your audience to think she is. In transmedia, every character is an unreliable narrator—but "unreliable" in the sense that each character will be trying to get your audience to think of her in the way she wants to be seen. There can be a gap between what a character is saying and how she says it, and in that gap, character can shine through.

Some examples: Characters who insist they aren't the kind to hold a grudge, but who take every opportunity to talk smack about the people with whom they've feuded with in the past. Characters who talk long and loud about how great their life is, and let slip the barest mention of a major looming conflict or worry in an offhand way. This sort of mismatch isn't going to be necessary or even advisable for every character or every project, but used well, it can create a wonderful depth to the people in your story.

Conveying Dialogue Online

Using the real world and Internet as a narrative platform creates interesting issues concerning how to reveal communication between characters that would be private if they were real people. Sometimes your story needs to reveal this information to the audience . . . but how? Fortunately, there are several well-established methods to deal with this.

For our purposes, let's look at two basic categories: dialogue between two or more characters, and dialogue between a character and the audience.

Conveying dialogue between two or more characters that occurs without the audience being in on it can be tricky. Assuming that you don't have a web series, a graphic novel, or some other traditional single-medium outlet for your multiple-character interactions, then you need to establish under what conditions the dialogue occurred and how you want to propagate it. Here are the most common situations:

1. **Public conversation over digital media.** This is arguably the easiest possible kind of dialogue to convey. You can do it as though it were really happening, with characters exchanging @ replies on Twitter, or alternating comments on a forum, blog, Facebook post, photo, or any other platform that allows comments. Just be very careful not to use the wrong account inadvertently—this is an easy mistake to make, and audiences tend to forgive it easily, but it's definitely a rookie blunder.

2. **Private conversation on digital media.** This can be a little harder, depending on the conventions you're using for your story. Strictly speaking, if you're posting private recorded content online under the guise of one of your characters, you need to think about why your character would reveal that information to the audience. Your character needs a defined motive for spilling those secrets, so conversations in which the two villains are conspiring, for example, will take more legwork to explain away.

   Interactive components often come to the rescue here, allowing the players to "work" to obtain access to information that they shouldn't rightly have. As a result, you get mechanics like the hacked email account, the critical security flaw in the company intranet, or the mysteriously sourced security camera footage. These tropes are widely overused, though, and have lost their potency with time. Use them sparingly, if at all.

   It's also possible to create and use an outlet for secret content to be revealed under the auspices of a narrator (or in some other omniscient-third-person fashion). If you plan to do this at all, you have to begin from early on in your story. When you haven't provided that space from the get-go, suddenly shifting gears will feel disruptive, implausible, and lazy.

3. **Live conversation.** There is a third category for conveying dialogue in which public vs. private doesn't quite apply: dialogue between two characters who are just talking in person or on the phone, the traditional way. Almost all dialogue in traditional single media happens this way—novels, films, video games.

In this case, your options for conveying dialogue amount to posting video or audio of it from one of your characters (thus bringing it into one of the digital media categories), arranging for it to take place during a live event and ensuring that it will be eavesdropped upon by players (and hoping they tell the wider audience), or having a character report the conversation later on in another medium.

If you choose to have a character describe a conversation after it's occurred, you don't have to convey the specific words spoken at all, as you would in traditional written dialogue. If it's in keeping with the character's established voice, then of course you should. But you can also stick to describing the end result of the conversation: "Me and my blue-ribbon pumpkin muffins had a friendly chat with Chester next door. Don't think he'll be letting that dog of his out from now on."

Dialogue with the Audience ‿

Dialogue between your characters and the audience is much easier to execute from a structural point of view than dialogue between characters, but it takes much more discipline and endurance to follow through adequately.

It's simple enough on the face of it: you just talk to your audience, then listen, and then respond, all in character. You can use forum posts, or comments on blogs, Flickr, or Facebook. @ replies back and forth on Twitter. Email exchanges. IM messages. The platforms you use are the social media choices you've already made for the character.

When it's done well, this gives your audience that deep illusion of reality, and a suspension of disbelief far beyond what a single-medium story can offer. Dialogue between a character and the audience has limited narrative use, though. It's a weak and poorly scaling vehicle for advancing the plot; you can't be sure what your audience will say to you, and whether you'll get the openings you're looking for.

Worse, if it's private communication (like direct email exchanges), it's possible that large swaths of your audience will miss it entirely. Players who don't participate (or worse, don't even realize that there's something to participate in) might lose track of the story's progress as a casualty. If that happens, you'll lose them as audience members.

Purely from an engagement perspective, allowing and using dialogue directly with your audience is irreplaceable. Nothing else provides the same intensity. And if you're making an interactive experience, this kind of two-way dialogue can be instrumental in setting challenges and shepherding your players through the story. (Though just as often, it's one-way dialogue masquerading as responsive interaction.)

But it's a good bet not to rely on truly responsive two-way dialogue, especially for key plot points, and especially if you're aiming for an audience with more than a few thousand players. Always have a plan B.

Q&A: NINA BARGIEL

Nina Bargiel is a screenwriter who has worked on such transmedia projects as the Streamy-winning *Valemont* for MTV and Will Wright's *Bar Karma*. She is currently a writer on the Nickelodeon show *How to Rock*.

Q: *How did you get into transmedia?*

A: By pure chance, really. Stan Rogow, executive producer of *Valemont* and one of the cofounders of Electric Farm, needed someone to create the online experience for *Valemont*. He was my executive producer on *Lizzie McGuire*, and he remembered that I did this "Internet thing" (blogging), and so he literally called me up and asked, "Do you still do that Internet thing? Because I have a job for you." And suddenly I was in charge of creating the transmedia experience for *Valemont*.

Q: *Can you tell me a little about your favorite projects?*

A: I haven't done that many, but one that will always remain dear to my heart was my first one: *Valemont*. Is that cheating? That may be cheating. I think that if I had sat down and told a bunch of people what I planned to do, they would have looked at me like I had three heads. But since I had contacts only in the TV-writing world (and not the transmedia/web world), I didn't really have anyone to bounce my ideas off other than my bosses, who said, "Great, do that!" Plus having a first-person experience of seeing how the audience reacted to the content was incredibly rewarding, especially in the multiple instances where they began creating mini-*Valemont* stories of their own.

Q: *Where do you see the art and business of storytelling headed over the next few years?*

A: I hope that we figure out a way to monetize. I think transmedia seems to be either the GIANT BLOCKBUSTER ADVERTISING TIE-IN or the indie movie model. There are some projects that are in between, but not many. Proving that there is a business model for the middle ground will be conducive to the art and the business of it all.

I hope creators and storytellers will be more open to sharing their worlds so that transmedia has a chance to grow, but I also understand that there's a lot of trust involved in handing over your story to strangers.

Q: *What would you recommend that transmedia creators learn about to improve their craft?*

A: Participate. Read. Write. Get online and see what other people have done. If you want to create for a market, know what that market is doing and how it operates.

Q: *When you handle the social media presences of several characters at once, how do you keep them all distinct?*

A: First, look at the character profile. What would their profile pic be? What about their background? Their bio? Their username? I'm not a big fan of including the show name in character usernames, although in the link in the profile, I'd probably include a link to the in-show experience. (Or the show, if there's no in-show experience.)

Then there's how your character actually tweets. Think about things like time zones. Time of day. I was on the West Coast (PST) when I was tweeting for the *Valemont* characters (EST), and to make sure to keep the experience feeling "real," I had to adhere to an eastern time schedule, which meant getting up at 5 a.m. some days to start tweeting.

Also, each character should have a unique voice. I usually give each character a "quirk" to keep them separate. One character may never use contractions. Another might include a lot of u (you) and ur (you're), and another may use snippets of (bad) French, etc.

Q: How does your creative and production process change when you're making stuff up on the fly instead of going through rounds of revising first?

A: Most of my stuff has been made up on the fly. I usually start from a strict timeline/outline, and then fill in the blanks in between. While I've worked on bigger productions, I've been the main transmedia person for those productions, developing and running the entire creative experience, so as long as I adhere to the story and timeline that the original creators of the properties have set forth, I'm free to play as I please.

The funny thing is that this often creates more work because I'm committed to what I do, so I'll try out more things and be online more often. I also incorporate and react to the audience in real time. I think you can have more audience interaction if you have more flexibility to create on the fly, but I also realize that most property creators are scared to trust someone to this extent. I come from the TV-writing world, and I'm used to playing with other people's characters in a world I didn't create.

10

Conveying Action Across Multiple Media

Action is all the stuff that happens in your story as a result of the intersection between characters and motivations. If there is no action, then nothing is happening; if nothing happens, you don't have a story. So one of the primary tasks of a storyteller is to effectively and compellingly convey action.

We know how to convey action in video.

Indy makes another daring getaway
Raiders of the Lost Ark™ & © 1981 Lucasfilm Ltd.
All rights reserved. Used under authorization.
Unauthorized duplication is a violation
of applicable law. Used courtesy of Lucasfilm Ltd.

We know how to do it in comics.

Iron Man turning the tables in a fight
Iron Man © and TM Marvel and subs.
Used with permission.

We even know how to do it in flat text.

At that instant the cottage door was opened, and Felix, Safie, and Agatha entered. Who can describe their horror and consternation on beholding me? Agatha fainted, and Safie, unable to attend to her friend, rushed out of the cottage. Felix darted forward, and with supernatural force tore me from his father, to whose knees I clung, in a transport of fury, he dashed me to the ground and struck me violently with a stick. I could have torn him limb from limb, as the lion rends the antelope. But my heart sank within me as with bitter sickness, and I refrained. I saw him on the point of repeating his blow, when, overcome by pain and anguish, I quitted the cottage, and in the general tumult escaped unperceived to my hovel.

—*Frankenstein*, Mary Wollstonecraft Shelley

Conveying action and urgency across multiple media, though, is quite a lot trickier to do.

SINGLE MEDIA

There's no reason you can't keep the heart of your action in your single-medium components; indeed, for Hollywood-style transmedia stories, this is the primary mode of operation. Films, books, video games, and comics all use their own native methods. Even stories that rely more heavily on social media can stick to single-medium storytelling for the main action by putting video clips of key action scenes on YouTube, publishing tie-in comics, and so on.

It's common for designers who are trying to make extremely immersive, feels-like-it's-really-happening drama to worry about the logistics behind each piece of media—who's making each piece of content available to the audience, and why. In that light, mixing and matching third-person-style content like books and films with social media elements might seem incongruous.

In general, though, as long as you're consistent with the structure you establish, the audience isn't much concerned with this. In the teen docudrama *Routes*, we fretted over creating a plausible reason for the characters to cut a weekly webisode together and post it online. We needn't have worried; nobody really cared.

Likewise, the transmedia narrative *Last Call Poker*, a marketing campaign for the Xbox game *Gun*, even included pieces of third-person narrative interspersed with character interaction. Again, the players didn't really notice, and they certainly didn't object to the different modes of storytelling being used. The fiction project *Shadow Unit* maintains episodic chunks of narrative text and real-time drama unfolding on LiveJournal, and it all weaves together smoothly without complaint from the audience.

As long as your story is good, your audience will accept the conventions you establish without even truly noticing them. So if you want to keep your action in

one medium and use the others more for character and worldbuilding work, more power to you.

ACTION OVER MULTIPLE MEDIA

It's possible, though, that you don't want to limit your action to flat media. Maybe you want to include interactive elements, or your platform of choice is social media; maybe you don't have the budget for big single-medium pieces and need to adopt a more DIY guerrilla style.

You can still get the job done, but you're going to have to dig a little deeper and work a lot harder. For each piece of action you have to convey, you're going to have to answer a few basic questions; once you do that, you'll have a grip on how to choose which media to use and how to use them. Here are the things you have to know up front:

1. **What is the action I'm trying to convey?** Whether it's a chat over tea, a daring break-in, or a massive explosion, the element you have in mind must be a specific event that takes place. If you're not clear on what that event is and how it plays out, you can't hope to convey anything else.

2. **Who knows about this event, and what is their motivation?** If you're using social media techniques, you can convey information only if that character would know about it . . . and would want to talk about it, too. Don't have characters spilling secrets they couldn't possibly know.

3. **How urgent should this event feel to the audience?** This ties into rising tension. The higher your tension should be around a piece of action, the more immediate your coverage should feel in order to provoke a sense of urgency.

4. **What is your audience's role in the event, if any?** Not every project or every event needs to be interactive, but you need to plan out precisely what the

audience's role is, whether it's phoning the hero in the nick of time or simply clicking on a link in an email to watch a video.

PICK YOUR POISON

Once you're clear about what you're trying to accomplish, you can move ahead with crafting a plan that achieves just that. Here are a few common options for conveying action:

1. **Live coverage.** For our purposes, *live* means that the action and the description of it are happening simultaneously. You can do this with, for example, a series of tweets, or with photos and video streamed or uploaded on the spot. If your action is "newsworthy," you can also use a series of breaking news updates. (Creating a fictional news outlet can be a profoundly useful tool; if it fits into the kind of story you're trying to tell, I highly recommend it.)

    Live coverage is great for lending immediacy and urgency to your action. But it can also require a volume and pacing of content that isn't sustainable for you, or for your audience—particularly not for extended periods of time. There's another potential drawback, too: you can't analyze an event as it occurs, and there's not much room for displaying a character's internal reactions, either. It's possible that you can lose some nuance as a result, unless you fill in extra character work after the fact.

    If you plan to use the live coverage technique, it's good practice to find a way to tell your audience when to be alert well ahead of time. If your audience doesn't catch something that happens live when it happens, they'll feel like they've missed out, and they just might resent you for it.

2. **Delayed coverage.** This means describing the event to your audience after it's occurred, not while it is allegedly happening. There are lots of tools you can use for delayed coverage: blog posts (in text or video), outbound emails from a character, and so on; delayed coverage is the typical currency

of social media. In a sense, the entire tradition of epistolary novels is delayed coverage; they involve a character describing events after they've happened, from conversations to close calls.

Delayed coverage is inexpensive to produce and generally fairly simple to distribute. It's fast and cheap to blog, "OMG I was mugged at the farmer's

PACE YOURSELF

Finding the correct pace at which to tell a transmedia story is both vitally important and deadly hard. You have to keep your tension rising at a steady pace and your stakes mounting; you have to create enough volume of content or frequency of installments to keep the audience satisfied, but not completely sated.

Too long between installments and your audience may forget about your story entirely, never mind care about it.

Too much and your audience will become overwhelmed and burn out (you're vulnerable to this, as well). It's also possible, unfortunately, to produce such a weight of content that new would-be audience members are frightened away before they really get started. This is especially the case with the traditional ARG. Its blurry outlines get in the way of the audience knowing where to start at all, much less how to catch up with the story in progress.

Franchise-style transmedia properties must consider pacing mainly in light of how quickly different big-picture components should be released. That's generally going to be the result of market and production factors, and not be very flexible, so the story has to bend to work with it.

If your story has a heavy television-based component, the pacing practically takes care of itself; the TV schedule will dictate it. Often this amounts to market, he had a GUN!"—especially compared with the costs of filming the same scene. And as another bonus, you'll get the opportunity to provide information that more immediacy would miss: "All I could think about was how undignified it would be to die at gunpoint while clutching a bag of Granny Smiths."

big weekly updates on TV, with other components being updated somewhere between once a day and once a week, plugging the gaps between episodes. It's common for the extended component of a TV show to go dark when the show is off the air, but it's also common to have a web prequel as a marketing campaign in the ramp-up to a season premiere.

More fragmented transmedia projects—your real-time social media dramas, ARGs, and live performances—can be even trickier to pace. But you can learn from looking at what works for all kinds of serial fiction. Daily, weekly, and monthly schedules can all work, provided that once you set the expectation, you stick with it—for the most part.

In general, the longer the delay between pieces of your story, the bigger those pieces should feel. Nobody wants to wait a year for a single photograph and a 50-word caption; likewise, nobody wants three new hours of video and 50,000 words of web content every single day. Once in a while, you can ramp up the volume of content for short bursts to provide a feeling of higher tension and intensity. But don't go completely radio silent without warning your audience, or you'll burn through a lot of goodwill.

And always keep in mind that you'll have to spin out your whole story with the resources you have available, whatever they may be (and no matter how much you have, you can always use more). Plan ahead so you never leave your audience hanging.

There is a downside, though. Delayed coverage can bleed any sense of immediacy from your story, and in turn can lower your perceived stakes and tension. That's because your character has implicitly survived to tell the tale. Still, not every piece of action in your story needs to be full-tilt and highest-stakes; you can use delayed coverage for the bulk of your action and rely on live coverage only for the few most significant events.

3. **Story archaeology.** In this method, you provide evidence that the action occurred offstage, then give it to your audience so that they can work out what happened themselves. This might include photographs of a crime scene uploaded to Flickr, a family tree, scans of notes passed in class, adoption records, a police citation for assault, security video footage of the crime scene—anything that conveys information can be a vector for conveying past action as well.

Creating evidence hits a sweet spot of conveying information in an efficient, scalable, and interesting way. It gives your audience something like fiero (the giddy rush of overcoming an obstacle) when they figure out what the evidence means and how it fits into the wider context of your story, and it maintains a high degree of immersion. It's terrible for immediacy, though, and it's best used for conveying elements of backstory or for revealing parts of the narrative that were hidden at the time that they occurred.

Be very, very careful of the friction problem, however. The more tiny pieces you break your story into, the harder an audience member will have to work just to understand what's going on. Evidence fabrication can be a powerful tool, but it should be used sparingly for the spine of your story, unless a high barrier to entry for a wide audience isn't a problem for you.

STRUCTURE

11

Fine-Tune for Depth or for Scale (Not Both)

*T*ransmedia's siren call to creators is as alluring as it is because of the tremendous creative possibilities it offers. But often, large chunks of your project should be determined by the purpose of your story and the resources you have available. The creative specifics of your story can have little or no bearing on the overall structure.

What platforms you use, how much content you create, and whether you fine-tune the story so that it is best enjoyed by a single player or by a community of participants will all affect what kind of audience you attract, and how deep into your story its members will go. All of these decisions are structural ones; they affect the overall shape of your story, like a skeleton, without dictating what the surface details will be.

Structure is dead important. No matter how innovative and compelling your story is, if it's structured poorly, nobody will ever know.

Every industry has its own version of the 80/20 rule. It's a blanket rule of thumb in business, and depending on which version you learned, it might be that 80 percent of your profits come from 20 percent of your customers. Or 80 percent of your problems come from 20 percent of your features. Or 20 percent of your employees do 80 percent of the work.

Transmedia has its own version, too: 20 percent of your audience is responsible for 80 percent of your activity. The specific numbers will vary depending on your project, of course, but the principle is sound: most of your participation will come from a small segment of your audience.

Often the audience is divided into three rough categories: 80 percent passive viewers, 15 percent engaged audience members, and 5 percent superfans. Passive viewers will follow along, but they won't do much beyond that. Engaged audience members will seek out new information and participate in some interactive elements of your story. The most highly engaged players are the ones who join forums to talk about your story, try to solve every puzzle, travel hundreds of miles to go to live events, create and update wikis or guides to your story, and so on.

Unfortunately, the more engaged groups are also the ones with the smallest numbers; hence the engagement pyramid.

That means that when you build a deep experience that requires a lot of audience initiative, it's possible that the lion's share of your audience will never see most of that content, and might not even know it exists. At the same time, the immersive feeling created by deep content is one of the key elements that make transmedia narratives exciting. There is an inherent tension between making a narrative that is very rich and deep, and making a narrative that scales to a larger audience but is shallow. This fundamental tension between depth and scale informs every structural component of a transmedia project.

Most artists would say without hesitation that their priority is to make something that has as much depth as possible. A locative art

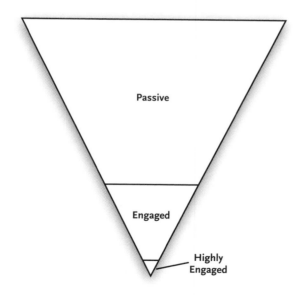

The engagement pyramid

narrative or a portfolio piece would benefit from making a richer experience for fewer people. A common method is including Easter eggs or chains of interaction—essentially locking away story-critical content behind barriers that require action from a player to overcome, like solving a puzzle or sending a text message to a character. That's not always a pragmatic approach, though. That's because there's another way to frame mass-market or shallower experiences—they're a lot more accessible.

Most businesses would say without hesitation that their priority is to make something as mass-audience and accessible as possible, and forget about depth. Sadly, this risks damaging the quality of your overall experience. Something that tries to engage everyone equally well can wind up engaging nobody at all. Still, designers working in marketing, for example, should carefully weight their experiences toward the broad-but-shallow end of the spectrum. That doesn't mean that you can't put in any deeper elements, but whenever possible, keep accessibility by even fairly passive audience members as your top priority. This means keeping the bulk of your content out in the open and telling players not just where it is, but how it all fits together.

Bear in mind that there's an interesting wrinkle on this that can occur in live, performative, or interactive transmedia projects. Sometimes, that top few percent of your audience who get the most from your story will actually become part of the story for everyone else. This can be formalized on your end, with phone calls, videos, or other submissions from your audience being cut in with your canon content, or with specific audience members getting a shout-out.

Even without that, in challenge-based games, the top few percent who are producing mind-blowing solves and unlocking progress for the whole community often become a part of the entertainment—that mass majority of the audience is watching the deepest, most involved players playing the game, on top of following the story itself. It can rise nearly to the level of a spectator sport.

Is it strictly impossible to do deep and mass-audience at the same time? No. No, but . . . there's another rule of thumb in most industries: you can get something done cheap, fast, or well; pick any two. The equivalent transmedia storytelling

pick-two-of-three is again a little different: cheap, deep, or mass-audience, pick two. It's possible to play to both ends of the rope and make a rich and very deep experience for an audience of millions, but it'll cost you. Know what your priorities are.

THE COST OF FRAGMENTATION

Many transmedia stories rely upon the audience's ability to collect and make sense of multiple story fragments—tweets, blog posts, and video footage, for example. But there is a distinct drawback to having a highly fragmented structure: the more fragmented an experience is, the more difficult it is for a mainstream audience to follow.

It takes effort to seek out that next piece of a narrative. Not always a lot, to be sure; sometimes it's a single click, one little Google search, or 10 bucks to spend on the next film or book. If you're switching media, that friction becomes a lot higher. People have an innate resistance to switching from watching movies to reading novel tie-ins. That same resistance keeps people from shifting from playing a video game to watching the movie version. A similar resistance will keep people from filling in a username and password to register for your site; it's easier just to close the window and not bother.

This friction erodes the number of players that follow you every time you switch media in a transmedia narrative. Still, there are techniques that allow a creator to tell an immersive and authentic-feeling story, while helping less sophisticated players to put the pieces together.

Let's say you want to create a very accessible story, but you don't want to sacrifice depth to do it. What specific actions can you take?

1. **Cross-link heavily.** This should be a no-brainer, but it's very easy to overlook. If you're creating a transmedia story with multiple websites, tweet streams, and so on, make sure to provide links from every one of these sites

to all the others. Or, better yet, create a single meta-site that is about your story but not a part of the story world itself. Use it to aggregate these links and take the work out of simply trying to follow the story for your players. If you do create a meta-site, it's then crucial that you link back to that site from every other location you use. Print the URL on your promotional materials. Put it in your credits. Make it absolutely unmissable.

2. **Provide rolling recaps.** It can be easy for people in your audience to lose track of what's happening in the story, particularly if they've inadvertently missed some pieces of content (or, for a real-time narrative, for audience members who come to the story midway through).

   It's a good practice to provide periodic recaps of the pivotal events in the story so far, as in TV with the "last time on this show" montages, or in long book series with a quick summary at the beginning of each book. You can also do this in the guise of a character, if so desired, particularly if you have a character who is serving as a guide (more on this in Chapter 13). But you can also sum up the story so far on a meta-site—the same one you use for cross-linking.

3. **Map out your intended audience path in a flowchart.** If at any point you are chaining content, so that (for example) you need to send Friar Lawrence an email before the star-crossed couple can have their secret wedding, then you need to be sure that the audience knows who Friar Lawrence is and how to find his email address. This is applicable not just to locked content, but also to revelations. Make sure you have a good grasp of what your audience learns about the story, and when.

   Trace those chains of discovery to make sure that every link is present and obvious. If possible, have someone who doesn't know much about your story test out your content to make sure you've done a good job of putting signposts for your audience members so that they don't get lost.

STRUCTURAL CONSIDERATIONS

Here are a few questions to ask yourself while you're deciding how to structure your story across multiple media, and a few tips on how the answers to those questions should change your design.

1. **What is the purpose of this project, and who is it for?** If your purpose is to gather an email list, then submitting an email address should be a core activity that participants must engage in at some point in the story. If it's creating awareness of a social issue, make that the key conflict of your narrative. If it's telling a good story and making a little money, make sure you're creating something that's worth paying for. And always, always make sure that your project uses platforms and conventions that your target audience will be comfortable with.

2. **Should the story play out dynamically in real time, or should it be a static experience in which you can go back to the beginning and start over at any moment?** Real time creates a very immersive and immediate feeling, and is much better for obtaining publicity or community building. You do risk creating a barrier to entry for audience members who missed the beginning, though, and once it's over, you need to either restructure it or accept that it's over. Which one you choose will often be decided by your overall goals for the project.

3. **How high a barrier to entry am I putting up?** Requiring registration, locking content behind challenges, and requiring high-end technology are all elements that can immediately erode your potential audience. That's not to say you should never do these things; there is often a good reason to require registration—for example, if you're making a single-person narrative and need to track progress over multiple media through that login. And if part of the purpose of your game is to promote a new technology, then it's only natural to use that technology, no matter how much (or how little) market saturation it's achieved. Just be cautious about what it is you're asking your audience to commit to.

WHAT MEDIA SHOULD I USE?

In an ideal world, the media you'd choose to use would be the ones that serve the story best. Bam, you're done. Unfortunately, in the real world, we have to be a little more pragmatic and take into account a giddy whirlwind of factors, from time and budget restrictions to audience sophistication, accessibility, and scale.

Your audience should influence which media you use. A great transmedia campaign uses the platforms its target audience already calls home, and doesn't use the ones that the target audience thinks poorly of or doesn't have access to at all. Just as an example, a project for tweens that requires access to cutting-edge technology is limiting its audience out of the gate. Tweens might not have access to the latest smartphone or iPad, and aren't likely to have the resources to acquire one, either.

Almost every individual or company will start out stronger in the creation and production of one medium over others. You need to play to your strengths. If you and your team have a filmmaking background, then focus on that and make as much mileage with it as you can: create a core film component, then add on episodic web content or unlockable video in a mobile application.

If your background and strength lie in text, then stick with that. Focus on books, blog posts, emails, and updates on social media. If you come from a traditional gaming background, focus on points of interaction and interlinked games small and large. If theater is your strong suit, then build an experience rooted in a live performance or a series of live performances, with elements that extend outward from there.

Most transmedia projects tend to be grounded most solidly in a single medium anyway, with other components acting more as satellites orbiting the main event than as entire stand-alone projects. That may change in time, but for now, there's absolutely nothing wrong with sticking to what you know best.

That's not to say that you shouldn't try to stretch to include more and different media every time you design a new project. You should, absolutely! Every platform brings something else to your project. Tentpole pieces like TV, books, and

film create solid revenue streams, of course. Social media and the web are excellent for allowing interaction, or the feeling of interaction, even with millions of people. Splashy live events make for fantastic publicity. But don't feel obligated to include any medium if you don't realistically think you can pull it off, or if it won't add anything to your story.

12

Special Considerations for Blockbuster Transmedia Franchises

Some of the world's most beloved transmedia projects are mammoth undertakings that include feature films, novels, comic series, and video games—in short, franchise entertainment. The most successful franchises are the ones where there is space for the audience members to imagine themselves as part of that world. *Harry Potter, Star Wars, Lord of the Rings*: these are all worlds that are very much bigger than the action on the main stage.

One of the amazing things we can do with transmedia is allow fans to have a place where they belong in a story world that they love. So it's a natural fit for franchise entertainment to move more and more in the direction of transmedia storytelling.

The much-lauded *Why So Serious?* campaign for *The Dark Knight* was an enormous stride in that direction. It's garnered awards, huge amounts of press coverage, and incredible fan love. And why is it such a big deal? It's because it took a world that did not have space for an audience to live inside it—Batman's Gotham—and created canon spaces where, for the first time, players could imagine themselves fitting. They became voters and accomplices. It turned a property that previously had not been very well suited to a transmedia experience and created one that suddenly was; the world wasn't just Batman and his allies and enemies anymore.

There is a common criticism of such extended experiences for entertainment franchises. It suggests that they don't create new fans; they merely service the fans that a property already has. That's probably true. But it's not entirely fair, either. All of that fan energy and excitement generated by a transmedia experience brings more people into the fold. The person who was sent a Joker mask by the campaign was very likely already going to see the movie, but maybe his roommate wasn't going to, or his cousin, or the person he enthused about the film to at work or at the coffee shop or on the bus. Those people, exposed to that catalyzed fan energy, are then more likely to become fans, too—or at least check out the movie when it hits theaters. Exciting your fans makes them contagious.

You probably have some examples of this in your own experience. I know I started reading *Harry Potter* because of all of the fan energy around it; that's also why I read *Twilight*. Giving your audience a focused outlet for its passion leads to a conversion of peripheral audience members into fans, and people who were never a part of the core audience into peripheral audience members. Participation is the engine that drives fandom, and fandom drives a story's success.

Not every franchise will be a good fit for transmedia expansion, though. The first *Twilight* book, for example, was poorly suited to it; there wasn't much of a world there outside of the couple in love. But it's a problem that can be fixed. Subsequent books in the series increased the scope of the world more and more, fabricating group dynamics and government structures that add up to a world bigger than just Bella and Edward and their true, sparkly love.

There are particular challenges that come with making such a goliath transmedia project. For one thing, you need to maintain consistency across all of your media in terms of story continuity, look and feel, overall tone, and, of course, quality.

It is absolutely crucial to the long-term health of a big transmedia franchise to make sure that every single audience-facing component is consistent with your story world's themes and canon. Story bibles and an integrated creative process help to make this possible.

STORY BIBLES

If you could have a single visionary executing every single project in a story universe, that would be ideal. Eventually, though, a world gets beyond the scope of a single person's creative vision, and yet consistency has to be maintained. Hence the story bible. The purpose of a story bible is to make sure that teams of creators who may not get to communicate with each other directly are nonetheless on the same page.

At a bare minimum, a story bible should include the same kinds of information you'd want in a Wikipedia article—who the main characters are and their defining characteristics, plus a summary of the overall plot. At best, it's an encyclopedic reference to everything about your story and the world it takes place in. You might want to include:

- Every scrap of information specific to your story world. A story bible for *Star Wars* would have to describe the Force. Other specific information might include maps, location descriptions, corporate profiles, family trees, and wildlife guides. If something is different from our own world, that information belongs in the bible.

- An index of every single piece of canon material in existence or in production, and where to find it. No scrap is too small: Twitter streams and feature films alike should be listed, each with a little bit of context about that piece's relationship to the greater story world, what characters appear in it, and a plot summary.

- A timeline that includes significant events in your universe and what time periods are covered in which pieces of media. It's all right for chronology to be a little ambiguous overall, but you'll need to be clear about the relationships between the fragments. (This isn't as important if you're planning on sticking to a single iconic state throughout your story.)

- Secrets and upcoming revelations. The story bible should include every important fact, no matter how secret it is from fans. It's not the place to be coy and hint at something. If Bob is the crown prince of Valrhania, but he won't find out until after another two films and a year of comics, it still needs to be in there. That information could affect creative decisions across the board.

If it's possible, creating a digital and searchable version of all your media is a huge help: books, scripts, blog posts, tweets, everything. Visual reference materials, too, are useful. Photos of actors, sets, costumes, concept art, and other art assets can become a visual library for future reference and maintain visual continuity.

A story bible isn't enough, though. It's a step in the right direction, but the weakness of a story bible is in that area where the story is still being fabricated. If the tale of a character's first kiss has never been told, the teams from two branches of the same universe might notice that opportunity at the same time and use it in completely different ways. That's the sort of conflict in canon that fans find deeply upsetting.

So it's even better if you have a continuity manager along with your story bible (or, if necessary, a small team of continuity managers). The continuity manager can act as liaison between disparate creative teams to make sure that no significant conflicts arise during production.

Companies like Starlight Runner Entertainment even specialize in helping to map out plot threads and story lines—sometimes years ahead of production.

Not only does this significantly reduce the chance of a major, glaring continuity error, but it also allows a sprawling franchise to map out precisely where any elements of intertextuality will lie, resulting in a more integrated and vibrant narrative thread.

FIRST THINGS FIRST

Some creators believe that you have to write your story bible before you can get to work on your actual story. On that front, I'm very much a story bible naysayer. In fact, I've worked on only two projects for existing properties that came furnished with a story bible at all! In lieu of that, I've relied on referring to scripts and photo galleries, or sometimes even fan-created reference material like wikis. (Don't scoff at the idea of fan reference works; these volunteer efforts can be more accurate and more comprehensive than anything you'd have the time or resources to make yourself.)

That's not to say that there isn't a time and a place for a story bible; any universe that passes that key threshold where it no longer fits into a single person's head definitely needs one. But it's something that can happen just as well at the tail end of the creation process.

If you get bogged down in defining the minutiae of a universe's flora and fauna or city names, that's time you aren't spending on defining the characters and conflicts that make your story interesting. If you're prone to forgetfulness, then yes, of course you can and should keep notes on important story elements as you fabricate them, or as you think of them.

But just as you don't need to make an entire transmedia project all at once, you also don't need to fabricate an entire story universe in one fell swoop. It's OK to start with just one story and fill in the reference materials later on. Leave yourself plenty of room in your world to expand into for now, and you can shoot for the moon later.

Q&A: CAITLIN BURNS

Caitlin Burns is a transmedia producer with Starlight Runner Entertainment, where she's worked on blockbuster franchises like *Avatar*, *Pirates of the Caribbean*, and *Transformers* for clients like Disney, Microsoft, Coca-Cola, and Hasbro, among many others. She is also working on an indie transmedia film project called *Jurassic Park Slope*.

Q: *Where do you see the art and business of storytelling headed over the next few years?*

A: No matter what you call a multiplatform project, whether it's a single story arc or a super arc that encompasses seven years of a franchise, transmedia storytelling is here to stay. The challenge that is ahead of the industry now is figuring out how to plan for both short- and long-term applications of the concepts to make better stories that allow for more creators to be involved in the creative space of a project. This is something that successful creative visionaries, like the Camerons, Bruckheimers, Lucases, and Spielbergs, already know: they are the ones who control the story, who have the big picture, but they can't be everywhere at once, and they can't physically make every decision on every platform of every story in their universe. The same problem applies to smaller projects that are just getting into multiplatform spaces. The harsh reality is that a filmmaker is not a game designer, a comic book writer, or a novelist. They need one another to create a project of a certain scale.

Story is the through line; no matter what industry your experience is in, you're human, and you understand a good story. Coproductions and increasing collaboration are the ways through the storm.

The final frontier keeping entertainment lawyers up at night is that the audience members, the fans, are a creative community in their own right; they desire and expect immersive experiences that allow their voices to be heard by the stories they love. Not only this, but they want places where they can flex their creative muscles as well, contributing new ideas to the story world in a tangible way. The creators at the helm will have to consider them as stakeholders in their story world just as much as the filmmakers, game developers, and novelists who are under contract to build the narrative, or ignore them at their peril.

Q: *Starlight Runner is without exception the authority in managing sprawling transmedia properties. What tips or techniques would you offer to a creator who is trying to get a handle on a big universe? Are there any special tools to learn?*

A: The real trick to dealing with groups on other platforms is to be able to speak about the story first. No matter what the intricacies of development on a specific platform are, the story will have to emerge there somehow. Story is the keystone for all of the interlocking projects. Get familiar enough with the story that you can talk about it in a platform-neutral manner.

The second big tip is to write stuff down. Once these projects are up and running, there will be lots of creative conversations, not only in set business meetings, but at lunches and dinners, or randomly when someone is stuck in an elevator or in the shower. Being able to write down the ideas that come up before those ideas are lost is key, and getting into the habit of doing so is vitally important so that these insights can be shared, remembered, and referenced down the road.

Q: *We hear a lot about Starlight's story bibles—what belongs in a bible like that, and what do you think should be left out?*

A: Ah, the Mythologies; what they are is encyclopedic references to the entire story world. In addition to some super-secret analysis that I can allude to only vaguely, this is where you want to put as much reference as possible for people, places, things, and concepts that are important to the story world. An important takeaway about this type of document is that it has a lot of details that aren't necessarily vital to what is going on at the moment, but that might turn into stories down the road. The other take is that they're platform-neutral; anyone working on any platform can make use of them regardless of specialty or background.

Q: *How do you manage a project with several creative teams to make sure all the pieces feel related?*

A: Again, this all goes back to story; if you've done your work and know your story, the story becomes your guide. If it feels like you're pushing the boundaries of your canon, you have to be able to look at the actual research you set down and defend why you would or would not move in that direction. If you can make a strong creative choice and defend it with research to back it up, then you are golden; if you can't find a good reason to do what you're doing, then at least you have a real sense that you may be going off the rails.

13

Interactivity Creates
Deeper Engagement

Some people consider interactivity to be a basic hallmark of transmedia storytelling. Bringing up interaction when you're talking about transmedia is like mentioning teeth in the context of eating: it's not a strictly necessary component, but there's a very strong connection there.

But people can also mean a lot of different things by that one word *interactive*. You might use it as shorthand for "uses the Internet," or to mean "the audience influences the outcome." Neither of these is strictly necessary for a transmedia narrative, as the big franchise projects amply demonstrate.

There is another definition, though, along the lines of "requires or allows audience action to learn more about the story." Interaction in this sense is an emergent property of transmedia. Allowing your audience to interact with your world can add tremendous depth of

engagement. So let's look at how to structure your narrative so that the audience has things to do, not just things to consume.

There are several degrees of interaction that you can build in, starting small (asking for minor seeking behaviors, such as going to a website that was mentioned on a TV show) and ending big, with the audience itself creating broad pieces of the story, as in projects like *World Without Oil* or *Cthalloween*, which are largely audience-written. You should be careful about how much you're asking your audience to do, of course; as shown by the engagement pyramid, the higher your barrier to participation, the fewer participants you will get.

It's possible to structure an interactive transmedia experience to allow a completely passive mode (reading blog posts, watching videos, reading tweets) and have an audience that does only that, without ever sending emails, leaving comments, or otherwise reaching out and touching the story world. What's more, this passive method of consuming a transmedia experience is the one that by far the most audience members engage in.

But for many of us, interaction, and particularly direct communication with characters, is the heart and soul of a well-built transmedia experience. It's what electrifies the audience. Even that silent majority of passive audience members can be electrified by the spectacle of other, more active participants reaching out and seeing the story reach back. It makes a world and a story come alive like nothing else.

What you may lose in player numbers, you will almost certainly make up for in depth of engagement for the players you keep. To split the difference, I prefer to structure narratives so that there is plenty of opportunity for the audience members to take action, but they are not punished by missing key plot points if they remain passive.

The tools of interaction are many, but they can be summed up in three basic categories: story archaeology, communication, and causing a change in the story world.

Story archaeology is a very glamorous term for how you consume a story that has been broken into fragments so small that none of them make sense on their own;

you have to find them all and piece them back together, like a piece of ancient pottery. Structuring a narrative in this sense is meant to create seeking behavior: mentioning a URL or social media profile within the main content on one platform to drive traffic to and interest in another, for example.

An offline equivalent is in the physical component of *Cathy's Book*, where the evidence packet included with the book (birth certificates, pictures, and letters) adds context to the main story, once the reader figures out how all the pieces relate to one another. This inspires a feeling of accomplishment in the audience members when they understand what's going on.

Communication is just what it sounds like: allowing the audience to communicate with the characters (or other entities) in your story, often on a forum or via social media, but sometimes also through the telephone, email, text messaging, faxes, and so on. This can be a simple back-and-forth exchange of information, but it can also be a vehicle for role-playing.

Communication can be outbound or inbound—that is, it can be you talking to the audience or the audience talking to you (or both). If you plan to be responsive in sending outbound communication, you're going to have to give some careful thought to the volume you expect to see and what resources you allocate to handle it.

The benefit, though, can be enormous. It allows the audience to feel a deeper connection to the story world. Your characters become more than fiction, instead rising to the level of people your audience knows and has a personal relationship with.

Finally, you can allow the audience's actions to *change the story world*. Particularly if you're planning on creating an actual game or incorporating game mechanics into your transmedia project, you'll need to create the feeling that the player's choices are having an impact on your story.

In most cases, it's a mistake to let your audience actually dictate how your story goes. As the adage goes, *Hamlet* doesn't become a better play if you let the audience vote on the ending. (There are exceptions for the kinds of narrative where the designer is providing a framework and the audience is creating the story itself; this is discussed in the next chapter.)

The goal is often to create an illusion of interaction instead. If you provide enough moments where the players feel that they are having an effect on the story, then the whole thing becomes imbued with the impression that the players have affected the outcome, even if there was never a real alternative outcome—even if all the audience has affected were non-load-bearing plot points.

One way to do this is to gate content so that the story doesn't progress until the player or players have achieved a goal, be that winning a high score on a minigame, emailing a character with the villain's plot, or picking up a ringing pay phone. For our *Romeo and Juliet* example, you could gate the story so that nothing happens until the players have persuaded Friar Lawrence to conduct the secret wedding.

You can stall the story until the goal is met, so that the story simply doesn't move forward until the desired player action is taken; you can prevent this from feeling like being stuck in place and convert it to a feeling of rising tension by having your characters communicate in increasingly desperate tones how important it is for the player to complete that interaction. This technique is often used even in traditional video games.

Alternatively, by building failures into your plan ahead of time, you can allow a failure state to exist that feels crushing but doesn't affect the overall course of your game.

REDUNDANCY

The perils of including an interactive component are that nobody will interact with it, or that they'll engage with it on different terms from those you'd envisioned. This is a very real risk, unfortunately; no matter how much planning and testing you do, you can't predict what individuals or communities will actually do once they come into your game.

You should consider this a feature, not a bug. It's exactly this feeling of unpredictability, even if it's only regarding surface details, that makes participation so rewarding.

But you can't let the unexpected hold your narrative hostage—particularly if you have several independent pieces of media all hinging on the same few plot points.

It is therefore absolutely crucial for you to build in tons of redundancy—if you really need the audience members to know that Mr. Jones was murdered by Miss Smith, then you can't construct the story so that the only way for them to find out is through an encrypted message that he scrawls on the wall in his own blood as he dies. Too much can go wrong that way. You might make an encoding error, so that the message winds up saying nothing or the wrong thing; or you might have a group of players who simply can't work out the puzzle, or who never notice the bloodstains on the wall in your carefully composed photograph. And if Mr. Smith was the only one who knew, and now he's dead . . . you're stuck, and your story is effectively derailed.

So it's much better practice to always have a plan B. In this example, you can try your bloody writing, but also have a backup plan where Mr. Jones had suspected Miss Smith of planning to do him in all along, and the players stumble upon his diary later. Or allow security footage of the dirty deed to come to light. Make sure that you always know how to rework your story to get to the same place, even if any single component fails. (Even better, plan for what to do if everything fails—better safe than sorry!)

There are other reasons to build in redundancy, too. If you're planning on sending out key narrative information by giving it to only a handful of your audience members—say in a mailing, at a live real-world event, by sending out physical artifacts, or through private email—you have to account for attrition. If you send one hundred gorgeous, unique clues to one hundred clever, high-profile bloggers, you're gambling that all one hundred of those clever, high-profile bloggers will actually write about what you've sent them. Unless you have a prior relationship that you're absolutely sure you can bank on, this isn't going to work. It's better to have four or five gorgeous clues to send to one hundred bloggers. It's better still if even those four or five clues cover much of the same ground.

ROLES AND GUIDES

In an interactive story, your audience needs to have a part to play, and both of you need to know what that part is. In some video games, this is a literal part to play, like an actor—the player stars as Super Mario, Master Chief, or the Grey Warden. The world reacts to the player as though she were that character; that means you don't have to know much about your real player.

There are multiple reasons why that might not fly, though, for a transmedia narrative. First off, one of the draws of transmedia methods is that you can transform your story into a social experience. But there's a certain cognitive dissonance in having a million people playing side by side, each one believing he is the one true James Bond. Assigning your players to a group identity instead gives them context for their own place and motivations in the story world.

Some projects are very literal about this—the audience is assigned to be an employee of a particular company, a member of a secret society, or an agent for a spy group. Some are less literal; you might be a "friend" of a character, as in *The Beast*, where the players were all friends of Laia Salla, whose friend has been murdered.

Earlier in this book, I talked about assigning the audience to the role of the Nurse in *Romeo and Juliet*. But that doesn't mean that each audience member is the same solitary Nurse. You could do that if you were making a single-player experience, of course. But if your creation is meant for a community, you must divest the role of individuality—strip it down for its parts, like a car in a chop shop, and allow the audience to collectively play that part as Juliet's circle of friends.

It doesn't matter precisely what the relationship is; what's important is that you ground the players in your story world and give them something to care about. Once you tell them what their connection is to the story in progress, they gain a sense of what their relationship is to the characters and events of your story—this is necessary context.

But simply telling the audience what its role is isn't sufficient. It's also good practice to provide the audience with a character whose role it is to guide the

ALWAYS REWARD EFFORT

There is a famous scene in the 1983 film *A Christmas Story*. The lead in it, a boy named Ralphie, has finally received the Little Orphan Annie decoder ring he sent away for. He can at last understand the coded messages that Annie sends out at the end of each episode of her radio drama! The moment arrives: he jots down the code, locks himself in the bathroom, and works furiously to decipher the message. It's an advertisement: "Be sure to drink your Ovaltine." His reaction is anything but a renewed dedication to Ovaltine.

The lesson here for a transmedia creator should be obvious: any time you are asking your audience to put forth effort, you need to reward that effort in kind. If you're asking people to solve a puzzle, you should unlock new content, or if you're using an overt game mechanic, reward them with points and badges. If you're asking for an extraordinary outlay of time and energy, like asking them to show up at a physical location on a particular date and time, the reward should be just as extraordinary.

And make sure you're giving the people in your audience something that they want, not just something that you want them to have. There is no quicker way to alienate an audience than to make its members feel that you're wasting their time.

audience through the interactive experience. The audience's relationship to this guide can vary quite a lot; players have been friends with the guide, employees, or co-conspirators. Often the guide is the protagonist in the story, and the story's key conflict is the problem that the audience is trying to solve, from locating stolen cars in *Art of the Heist* to helping a robot find true love in the indie project *Must Love Robots*.

The guide doesn't need to be a character—Lance Weiler's project *Pandemic* didn't have one, for example. But that project did have a robust infrastructure that was explicitly outside of the story world, including data on the progress of the game. That served the same purpose: making sure that there was a place for the audience members to turn when they weren't quite sure what was going on, or what to do next.

Creating interactive moments or even a whole real-time story can be a powerful tool, for all that it requires is careful planning. It doesn't have to be difficult. Despite my dire warnings, you can definitely learn and adapt on the fly.

Be realistic about what can possibly go wrong, make sure you have a plan B, provide a way to tell your audience members what it is you expect them to be doing, make sure they'll get something out of playing along with you, and then . . . then, hold your breath and take that leap of faith. It'll be the most exhilarating leap of your life. Once you've done it, you'll never go back.

14

Uses and Misuses for User-Generated Content

I *have a confession to make. I kind of hate user-generated content (or UGC, as it's* called). If you're not familiar with it, it's a particular kind of audience participation. Sometimes it takes the form of audience-submitted photos, video, or writing; sometimes the audience is role-playing; sometimes audience members are taking the driver's seat in creating your narrative.

UGC is a great concept on paper. From an artistic point of view, it brings you closer to those in your audience and makes the resulting creation as much theirs as yours. Nothing makes an audience more interested in a story than a feeling of ownership. From a business point of view, it demonstrates depth of engagement, and it can even shift some of the costs of content generation from you to your players.

But (and here's the dirty secret) user-generated content often doesn't work very well—not on the artistic front, and not on the business

front, either. The main creative reason why will be evident to anybody who's ever edited a publication, browsed the low-view depths of YouTube, or spent time in a fanfiction community. User-generated content is, by and large, not very good.

We have amazing consumer tools for video and photography available nowadays, to be sure, but availability doesn't automatically create the skill to use them well. Film school still exists in a world of cheap camcorders. A third grader can string words together to make a story, but it takes years of education and practice to get to the point where someone who isn't related to you would want to read it.

And then, even if you get in some truly high-quality pieces from your audience, there's no guarantee that those pieces will mesh with your artistic vision. This is a significant concern for projects where user submissions can become part of your established canon. Some projects that rely heavily on UGC, like the experimental fiction project *Mongoliad*, vet contributions and award canon status only to the ideas that they particularly admire.

There is also vast potential for legal problems. Back in the 1970s, science fiction author Marion Zimmer Bradley created a world called Darkover. It was enormously successful. Over the next decade, she expanded that world, with dozens of books, and even a series of anthologies of short stories, many of them submitted by fans of her work. Everyone was happy.

Until 1992, that is. That year, one fan wrote a lengthy story set in Darkover and sent it to Bradley. What happened next is a little contentious, and the truth is hard to get at, but it's evident that Bradley's next novel had significant similarities to the fan's work. The fan accused Bradley of plagiarism and demanded monetary compensation and coauthor credit on the book. In order to avoid a legal headache, the publisher ultimately declined to publish Bradley's book at all. As a result, many authors now have a blanket policy of never reading fan fiction or fan contributions.

This is bad enough when it's one author losing months or years of work on a single book. A transmedia franchise might have a lot more at stake. Imagine if, instead of a book, it was the next tentpole film in your transmedia project, and you had partnership deals worth millions of dollars in place and hundreds or thousands of jobs riding on it.

The moral of that story: if you are going to accept user-created submissions, you'd better make sure that your legal terms for submission are completely airtight.

Aside from problems of legality and quantity, another enormous problem with UGC is that the vast majority of people simply won't ever bother to make anything for you in the first place. Asking your audience to create content for you is building an enormously high barrier to entry—you're requiring the members of your audience to have the tools to create content; confidence in their skills; and the time, effort, and desire to focus on you, instead of changing the channel, clicking over to a new tab, or fixing a sandwich. The more difficult participation appears to be, the fewer people will actually do it.

Here's an example. For nearly two years, we ran a weekly newspaper column contributed by players in the *Perplex City Sentinel*. We had tens of thousands of registered players, but even so, there were many weeks when we had no columns submitted. The barrier to entry was just too high. Even asking a player to fabricate a persona is asking him to make user-generated content. There are cases where collaborative worldbuilding works, but relying on it is a very, very risky strategy.

Think about the ratio of people who watch a TV show to the ones who write fan fiction about it, and then you'll get a general idea of how few people are interested in this kind of play. You can't just say, "Come build a world with me." You have to give an audience something to love and care about first.

HOW TO DO UGC RIGHT

UGC has to be treated with caution, but there are definitely projects where it can and does work. You just have to know how to do it. Reasons to use UGC despite the risks include creating activities for your players to participate in, creating points of interaction, fostering community, and even allowing your audience to create and influence canon.

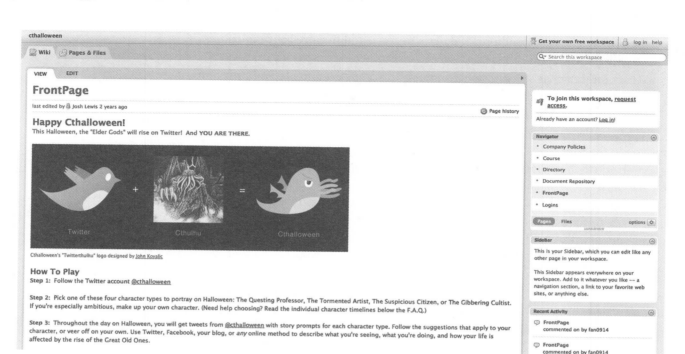

Cthalloween made participation easy

Often user-generated content will take the form of materials submitted to a single contact—a web form for an interactive challenge, for example, with submissions going into a gallery. In other cases, it allows the audience members to role-play along with you through platforms that they control, like social media, even taking their participation to their own blogs. Both of these methods share a virtue: players who are enthusiastic about the work they've done are likely to show their friends, potentially bringing in new audience members.

No matter how you plan to do it, though, here are a few key considerations for making it work:

1. User-generated content creates a tremendous barrier to entry. To encourage more participation, lower that barrier. Structure it so that each individual piece of content to be user-generated is tiny. Using the 140 characters of a tweet to participate in a project like *Cthalloween* isn't as much work as contributing an entire news column, for example, or crafting an entire fictional Internet persona. You can tweet once and still feel that you've been a part of the collective and collaborative experience.

   What's more, with a structure like *Cthalloween* had, you can still engage with the experience in a meaningful way as a spectator, even if you never submit anything yourself. I guarantee you that far more people watch the action on stage that other players are contributing than actively participate themselves. The engagement pyramid strikes again.

2. Ensure that there is no issue of maintaining a central canon and its continuity. If maintaining a clean and perfectly consistent continuity is necessary for you, UGC is definitely not the way to go. If you're set on using UGC, you'll need to either relax about inconsistencies or establish a specific space in your world where a "real" and conflicting truth will never be established.

   That way, each cluster of player-participants can spin its own interpretation of the story as they go along, and it won't matter. You can have six completely different origin stories and twelve accounts of what happened behind a particular locked door on the night of September 10. As long as everyone is having a good time, there's no harm done.

3. Spend some time with a lawyer to guarantee that you won't run into legal issues. If you'll be republishing UGC, you'll need to have very clear terms of service about what rights you claim on submission and what compensation your player-collaborators can expect, if any. And if you're allowing fans to create work outside of your own platforms, you'll need to be sure you're adequately guarding copyrights and trademarks.

There is more than one kind of successful UGC structure, of course; contest submissions often work, for example. Brain Candy president Scott Walker has experimented heavily with audience co-creation and even revenue sharing with his *Runes of Gallidon* project. And my own project *Floating City*, with Thomas Dolby, fostered an astonishing culture of UGC around patent submissions—players were given a framework to invent devices to exist in the world of *Floating City*, and when a patent was accepted, the player was rewarded with material advantages within the game. In this case, the rewards for participation were very high, even though the barrier to entry was also fairly high, so there was still a positive incentive for taking part.

And that's the real key to making sure that your UGC structure will work. It's very easy to ask your audience to create something because it would be fun or interesting for you to see what they come up with. But a good structure means that the audience will find the process of participating fun and interesting, too. There must be value on both sides of the equation.

Q&A: JAY BUSHMAN

Jay Bushman is a creator noted for his work under the banner of *The Loose-Fish Project*, which includes collaborative Twitter dramas like *#SXStarWars*, *Cthalloween*, and *The Talking Dead*, and an adaptation of the *Spoon River Anthology* as a group blog. He currently works at Fourth Wall Studios.

Q: *Where do you see the art and business of storytelling headed over the next few years?*

A: I really have no idea. It excites me—and scares me—no end.

Storytelling is like water—it will seep through any crack, find any conduit, conform itself to any vessel. As the number of media platforms and devices expands, and as people get more accustomed to how information moves all around us in a hypernetworked world, new formats for storytelling will only grow more diverse and widespread.

On the business side, I think we're going to see the continued decline of the major media monopolies as they fall victim to their sclerotic, siloed business models that cannot survive in a networked world. But I am extremely worried about net neutrality. Much of what independent creators (transmedia and otherwise) do on the Internet is predicated on access being equal. The loss of net neutrality would be a deathblow, pricing people out and killing the development and experimentation that we thrive on.

Q: *What would you recommend that transmedia creators learn about to improve their craft?*

A: Certainly, having a grasp of how things work on the Internet and mobile platforms is important, but I'd call that more of a general life skill at this point. You can research to learn about previous projects that are similar to yours, but beware. There's precious little to read about specific transmedia projects that isn't a marketing puff piece or just blatantly wrong. So don't accept things at face value.

Something else that would be invaluable to learn is really more of a habit to cultivate: keeping an open mind. The number of people who dismissed Twitter as trivial and self-centered is staggering, and yet people are using it to topple dictators, create art, and knit the world closer together. Every new tool and platform will always have a huge, immediate chorus of detractors screaming about how it's stupid, useless, or evil—and they'll want you to have an opinion too. Don't give in. Try everything. Explore. Play. Allow yourself to be surprised.

Q: *Why do you think some participatory projects succeed where others don't?*

A: I think the biggest factors in making a participatory project succeed are clarity, variability, engagement, and collaboration.

Clarity is the first and probably the most important—when potential new players first encounter your experience, they need to know exactly what they are being asked to do. Any confusion at this point is deadly, so save the nuance for later. And be prepared to explain it again and again. You're asking people to step outside their comfort zones, and many of them will be nervous and hesitant. Projects that do not have a clear arc are asking for trouble. Included in this is defining the duration of the experience. I've found that if people know how long something will last, they have a better feeling for how to pace themselves. I keep my projects short; I think the longest one so far has lasted six days. I find that players are more willing to commit to a short flurry of activity than to a long, drawn-out campaign.

Variability means creating a story world in which each player can have a unique experience and there are enough potential variations on the theme to interest a wide variety of people. For example, in my H. P. Lovecraft–themed *Cthalloween* project, I created a basic story throughline for the players to follow. But I also created four different character archetypes pulled from Lovecraft's stories and modified the throughline for each one. Players got to choose which of these types they wanted to play, and craft their stories along different story paths. (Also, it's usually a good idea to allow the option for people to play the bad guys. People love playing bad guys.)

Engagement means providing enough things to do and guidance for players who might easily get confused about what to do. This is where I think most corporate-based participatory experiences fall down: they provide for only a limited set of options, with infrequent feedback. It's very useful to have a main source of information to guide players throughout the experience. I also find it helpful to play a couple of characters myself and to recruit some experienced veterans to get involved. This helps model behavior for other players and can also be used to guide the story when necessary. This is a controversial practice in other types of transmedia experiences and ARGs. But I find it to be vital to these kinds of projects, and I think it's an important tool in providing a good experience for the people playing along. Even something as simple as recognizing a player's contribution reinforces for them that somebody out there is listening and that they are having an effect on the experience. Also, just because you're a creator doesn't mean you can't also have fun playing along!

Make sure to design ways to encourage people to collaborate with each other. Put players together in a virtual space and force them to interact. Design story paths that put them on a collision course. It's these instances of collaboration that people cherish and remember after the experience is over.

15 Challenging the Audience to Act

There are lots of reasons to incorporate puzzles and other more gamelike mechanics into a transmedia project. I call anything *requiring* player activity to move the story forward (above and beyond just consuming the media) a challenge. You might use a challenge as a sort of throttle for content, slowing the pace of the audience's movement through your narrative. You might use it to create a feeling of involvement in the story, giving the players a personal stake in the plot and its outcome. And maybe you want to create the illusion (or even the reality) of choice, to make the whole story feel less predetermined.

But no matter what your goal is, you're going to have to ask yourself a few questions during the design phase to establish a solid framework for your challenges. If you're not certain about these underlying criteria, you can't be sure your game mechanic is doing the work you want it to.

1. **What's the objective, and what's the reward?** Be very clear on why it is that you're expecting your audience to do the challenge at all. What's more, be sure you're conveying this information to the players. They need to have a motivation for jumping through your hoops. And on the other side of that coin, as with all interactive elements, make sure that the reward the players get for success is commensurate with the effort they are expending. This bears repeating several times, because it can be very easy to forget in the rush of production.

2. **Are my challenges meant for a single player at a time, or are they collaborative?** A single-player challenge is one that every player must complete independently in order to get the reward, like emailing in a correct response or winning a minigame. You can structure collaborative challenges in a few different ways. In one, a single player achieves the goal on behalf of a group, like answering a single ringing pay phone. In another, succeeding requires the collective action of a group of people working together, like answering ringing pay phones across several states on the same day.

    This is very much related to the question of whether the whole experience is meant for a single player or whether it's a community-driven, real-time performance; the structure of your challenges should match the structure of your overall story. And you should be aware of the distinction between competitive challenges (only the fastest 10 players get the reward) and collaborative ones, where everybody wins together. None of these structures is better than the others; they all have their uses. Make sure that the one you're choosing works with the story you're trying to tell.

3. **How hard is this challenge to solve or do?** The engagement pyramid strikes yet again: the harder your challenges are, the smaller your audience for them will be. I usually recommend skewing toward simpler puzzles for single-player experiences and for challenges that a player is likely to encounter early on. However, you can ramp up the difficulty level rapidly if you

can reasonably expect a community to coalesce around your experience, because the members of that community are likely to share answers—surprisingly, even if the overall game is competitive and prizes are at stake.

If your challenges are aimed toward collaborative action, you can make them quite a lot harder than you may realize. A community is smarter than all of the individuals who participate in it. Think of it this way: if you make a puzzle that only 1 percent of the population could ever hope to solve, and your audience consists of 10,000 players, that means you still have a hundred people in your community who can solve it. And in a collaborative structure, you usually need only one solver.

Some new puzzle designers will mistake an ambiguous puzzle for a difficult one. Ambiguity is the enemy. In a good challenge, when the player hits upon the right answer, you'll have provided enough clarity, hinting, and feedback that it isn't possible for him to be unsure whether he has the right answer. Don't leave any room for doubt.

4. **Is my challenge actually possible?** Check and double-check your puzzles to make sure they're solvable with the resources that you are providing, or that you can reasonably expect your audience members to get their hands on. And make sure that both the problem you're posing for your audience members and the way you expect them to solve it are readily apparent.

There are challenges that go against this, where merely working out what to do next is itself the challenge: unmarked and unintuitive interfaces, puzzles or games with no instructions, and the like. Use this technique sparingly, if at all; when confronted with uncertainty about how to tackle the problem, most of your audience will shrug and find something else to do.

It's a good practice to have a hinting strategy in place for collaborative and real-time challenges, in case your players get stuck, or in case some piece of crucial information gets lost in execution. Decide what you'll say, how long you'll wait to say it, and how you'll put the information in front of

the players. This kind of planning for failure states may seem excessive, but it's better to have a plan and not use it than to really, really need one and not have anything.

5. **How is the challenge relevant to the story?** In order for your entire project to feel like one single work and not a disjointed connection of unrelated pieces, the challenges need to feel like they serve a purpose in the context of your story. If you're asking players to decode a message, you need to know who coded it in the first place, and why—and they need to be able to figure it out.

   You can get around some of this by creating a character whose role it is to set challenges for the players (a villain, perhaps, or maybe someone who is taking the audience through some sort of testing regimen). Some transmedia projects go the extra mile and include puzzle trails or treasure hunts with overt prizes for the person who comes to the end first. That's possible only if the end goal for your challenge is directly tied to the conflict in your story.

REWARDS AND PRIZES

I'm not a big fan of giving out prizes like vacation packages, TVs, or shiny Apple devices as part of your game. For one thing, I feel that it cheapens the experience. It can come off as bribing people to participate, as if you don't have enough confidence in the value of the story you're offering.

It also has immediate implications for the tone and culture of your fan community. When prizes come into the mix, you begin to see more competition. Interestingly, if you break players into teams instead of having each individual player fend for himself, that competitive spirit gets even stronger. In extreme cases, it can manifest as outright hostility toward one another. It's not inevitable, but it certainly is a risk that you need to be aware of—particularly if you're using prizes in a hybrid design where you're also trying to create collaborative behaviors.

One of the biggest headaches of giving prizes, though, is that it requires you to impose a structure on your narrative that allows you to choose winners and define some behaviors as winning. This is problematic for stories where the bulk of your structure is aimed at passive behavior, or where you're aiming to create the feeling that your story is something that's really happening. Awarding 50 points to the player who emails the character with the correct combination to her friend's locker can be jarring, because it calls attention to the fact that your story is just a story at precisely the point when your player's suspension of disbelief should be most protected.

Last but not least, there are legal tangles that you get into when you offer a prize and officially become a contest or promotion in the eyes of the law. Suddenly you're subject to a bewildering morass of legislation about what you can do and how you can do it, mostly designed to prevent you from running an illegal lottery.

At the same time, it's understandable to want to reward your most dedicated participants, and on the surface, giving them cool swag seems to be a great way to do that. If it's an absolutely key part of your strategy, then you certainly can give out prizes; just be mindful of how you do it.

Sending out physical rewards as surprises is one way around the various legal and structural hassles. This means that you can't use the prize as a recruitment vector to get people interested in the game, but it also means that you can be somewhat arbitrary in deciding who gets rewarded and why.

This is a particularly nice touch if you're planning on giving out artifacts from your story world, not just merchandise like T-shirts or posters, because it makes the reward mechanism mesh smoothly with the story. From the player's perspective, receiving an apothecary's vial plucked from Juliet's apparently dead hand is going to be far more powerful and memorable than a smartphone that's going to be obsolete in a year or two anyhow.

You can also reward your highest-achieving and most-engaged players with content instead of with consumer goods. You probably don't want to separate your audience into two classes, with the group that never gets a prize having an inferior story experience as a result. To address that, you can reward your serious players with early access to content, rather than exclusive content. Similarly, you can reward the entire community by letting the first and most active players unlock content for everyone.

If you are promoting prizes as a recruitment tool, then be very clear about what kinds of behaviors are necessary to win. Is it recruiting on social media? Solving a puzzle the fastest? Whatever it is, make sure that the players absolutely know what they have to do. And if you do offer prizes, you'll need to consult with a lawyer to draft the rules of your game, and maybe even to help you administer it.

TYPES OF CHALLENGES

There is no end to the kinds of actions you can ask your players to take to meet a challenge in your game. Past games have required the audience to play a version of poker designed for cemeteries, write books, buy packs of gum, and decipher every kind of cipher and code known to man, from Morse to Enigma and back again.

The challenges that are going to work for your project will vary quite a lot depending on what kind of story you're telling and how you want people to interact with it. Given that the only limits are your resources and your imagination, I can't provide an exhaustive list. But here are a number of commonly used kinds of challenges that might inspire you:

- **Puzzle solving.** This has a dizzying array of possibilities in and of itself. There are your classic codes, ciphers, and encrypted messages, but there are also visual puzzles, word play, and spatial puzzles. They can be presented on a billboard, shown on the web, or projected onto a building. The difficulty with pure puzzles is integrating them into your story in a coherent fashion; it's very easy for this sort of challenge to feel tacked-on and irrelevant.

- **Contribution of content.** As discussed in the chapter on user-generated content, you can ask your audience to submit anything from videos to tweets in order to cause an event in your story. It might be contributing supportive video messages to make a character feel brave enough to take on a difficult task, or it might be garnering a benchmark number of tweets with your hashtag.

- **Real-world actions.** From picking up that ringing pay phone to surreptitiously snagging a dossier of top-secret documents from a covert agent on a street corner, real-world actions are a powerful tool. These can be difficult to execute and monitor, however, unless they happen on a very small scale—or unless you can partner with a chain, as *Why So Serious?* partnered with Domino's to deliver clues in pizza boxes.

- **Social engineering challenges.** This type of challenge requires the player to persuade a character to give her information or take an action on her behalf, be that inviting someone to a party or spilling the beans on who worked late on the night of the murder. These are elegant in concept but can be difficult to scale, because they require personalized interaction (or something that looks and feels like it) from an actor or a writer manning social media, a messaging account, a phone, or the like.

- **Story archaeology.** These challenges ask the player to follow a logic chain and deduce a story-critical piece of information, ranging from a login and password for a website to the identity of a murderer. This is more writing than puzzle design, up until the moment you require the audience to take action; rewards are often additional content. Audience members might use the information they deduce about a login form or in a phone system to gain access to a character's emails to read or voicemail to listen to, for example. Or they might be required to report the answer to a character, at which point the next part of the story unfolds.

- **Recruitment or social media messaging.** It's increasingly common to require a player to recruit friends into the experience in order to advance in the game. A closely related mechanism is requiring the player to tweet or post about the game for in-game rewards. The benefit to you is obvious: more players. But it's easy to go overboard with this and earn the contempt of the people you're trying to recruit; nobody wants to feel like they're being used as a marketing tool. Use this mechanism with caution, if at all.

- **Formal games.** You can, of course, use more formal games as your challenges, from browser games to street games. I like to use structured games as a metaphor for something occurring in the world of the story—a game of Sudoku as a stand-in for picking a lock, for example, or a point-and-click hidden object game as a stand-in for searching a room for a character's missing diary.

  Game design is a big topic, and one that I won't be able to adequately address here. In a sense, though, making a game mechanic is a lot like building a mobile to hang from a ceiling: you're creating a lot of little pieces that all have to balance together in a pleasing way when you're done. That balance is what makes or breaks your game.

Q&A: CHRISTY DENA

Dr. Christy Dena is a noted academic and transmedia writer, experience designer, and director whose work includes the 2011 Digital Emmy-nominated *Conspiracy for Good* and *The Hunt* for Cisco. Dena is currently working on *AUTHENTIC IN ALL CAPS*, an online comedy/drama.

Q: *How did you get into transmedia?*

    A: For me, "transmedia" is something I stumbled upon through my own creative practice. Although I had unknowingly embarked on it in the early 1990s with my multimedia theater projects, it wasn't until 2001 that a light suddenly went off. I had just written my first screenplay. It was a terrible piece of writing, but I had finished it, and the writer catharsis I went through gave me a new wave of hope. I knew the script wasn't something I could peddle professionally, but I was so enamored by the characters and their journeys that I started writing an adaptation. I rewrote it as a short and heavily symbolic folktale (as all folktales are).

I was also researching one of the characters from the screenplay, an agent. On the Internet, I discovered this thing called "software agents." Software agents, or chatbots, are pieces of software that you can program to have conversations with. This blew my mind. You mean I can write a program that talks to you? Yep. So I programmed the agent character, of course. Then I liked the idea of juxtaposing a contemporary character going through the same internal journey as the ancient folktale character. So I kept writing the short story about a teenage village girl, and interweaved that with a story about a teenage robot. At the end of each (print) chapter, there was a call to action to go to the website and chat with the character, then the bot prompted you to return to the book, and so on. As you can imagine, I immediately faced creative challenges that were unlike screenwriting, playwriting, or literature.

The creative challenge this project posed, and the fact that I could bring together two loves (the illuminated book and digital technology) were catnip to me. I searched high and low for a poetics of this strangely attractive way of writing and found nothing. It was then I decided that this was what I wanted to do.

I spent the next decade learning everything I could about this area: through researching, educating, and working with people in independent arts, branded entertainment, broadcast, film, gaming, publishing, theater, and dance. In the beginning there were no courses and it wasn't a widely known area, and so I got into what is now called transmedia by beating lots of bushes, charting paths, and answering distant whistle calls.

Things are different now. But I guess the point is, transmedia is a natural form of creative expression that I love. Your catalyst to entering this area will

guide your decisions about why you want to work in this area, what sort of projects you create, whom you choose to work with, and how you progress.

Q: *What would you recommend that transmedia creators learn about to improve their craft?*

A: I've found the minimum competency needed to work in transmedia includes understanding interactivity. You need to understand the basics of a feedback loop before you can understand transmedia. Since transmedia is about working across media platforms and/or art forms, you need to be crucially aware of the affordances and contextual use of the media you're employing. An acknowledgment of and respect for different art forms and their production processes will get you a long way. I could refer to lots of wonderful art forms and the reflective artist essays around them, but if I could say only one thing, it would be this: aim higher than what you see around you; aim higher than what is accepted as good and innovative; aim higher than what is comfortable to you.

Q: *What are the most important things to keep in mind when you're designing an interactive element?*

A: 1. Make sure the reward or outcome matches or betters the effort put in. I remember traveling for hours on trains and ferries to get to a live event for an ARG. What was there was exciting, but it didn't match the work I put in to get there. I always remember that experience and make sure I design elements where the effort doesn't exceed the reward.

2. Design for different behaviors. This isn't something that everyone does, and it doesn't have to be a design goal, but it is something I always do. I always work out what are (at least) the three main ways people can interact with my work, and I make sure that each one of these behaviors is addressed in a satisfying way.

3. Design for interactions that you would enjoy. It is so easy to get caught up in what other people apparently like and popular mechanics. But in the end, make sure you include the activities that you enjoy doing, and do them well.

4. Keep your theme in mind when making choices about interactive elements. If you design all your interactions, plot, and characters around the same strong, overarching theme, then you are making all the right moves to produce a meaningful work.

16

Make Your Audience a Character, Too

A transmedia project doesn't just have to manage its story and assets; it also has to manage its audience. Sometimes this is figurative, as in setting up and then fulfilling audience expectations. At other times it's more literal, as when you've created a forum and have to moderate the community.

The first step in any kind of audience management is getting to know who your audience is—if possible, figuring that out in the design phase and structuring your project to suit your target. This is an art all its own. You need to consider geography, culture, access to resources like smartphones, age, and literacy (both the old-fashioned kind involving reading, and digital literacy or other constellations of skills).

You can approach the process of acquiring your audience from either end. You can start with knowledge of the audience you want to attract and then do everything in your power to make your story interesting to those groups, or you can decide what kind of story you want to tell and then think hard about the natural audience that would be attracted to it and find it accessible.

Once you know who it is you're going after, you need to make sure you really understand them. Do you know how the people in your natural audience think? Do you understand their in-jokes? Do you know who their thought leaders are—and who their troublemakers are? If you don't, then you're going to need to do some research. Bear in mind, too, that your audience might consist of several different communities, each with its own subcultures.

There are multiple communities out there of gamers, cinephiles, theater aficionados, puzzle trail enthusiasts, and so on. Each one has its own culture and expectations. Especially when you're going to be creating something with interactive components or with a middling-to-high level of friction, you need to really get these communities, and preferably as an insider.

Geography also has an important role in structuring your project and your interactions, although the specifics of those differences are still largely unmapped. Anecdotes would suggest that South American audiences seem very enthusiastic about engaging in role-playing; American audiences enjoy competitive elements and puzzle solving; and European audiences tend to be most enthusiastic about attending live events. There aren't yet enough data in to see if those are accurate descriptions. Still, there's no doubt that cultural distinctions will emerge, and you'll need to keep an eye out for them.

Once you understand the people in your audience, it's easier to figure out what kind of experience they'll think you're promising, so that you can be sure to deliver on it. This can be more difficult than it appears at first blush—we want to preserve the feeling of surprise, but we also don't want players to get a completely wrong idea and be profoundly disappointed when they don't get something they thought they had earned.

This is a completely different kind of issue from that of surprising your audience with the twists and turns of your story. Nobody would argue that a plot twist coming out of left field is a bad thing. But if your trailer makes a film look like a tender love story, your audience isn't going to be pleased to find that it's actually a blood-spattered slasher flick.

Still, sometimes, despite your best efforts, you're going to let the audience down. In any system with as much potential for chaos as a transmedia story, it's inevitable.

Maybe your would-be audience has been following the countdown timer on a website, and at the last minute you replace it with . . . a new countdown timer, because of technical difficulties. Or maybe you inadvertently gave the impression that your project would be a big-scale three-month affair, but you catch your audience by surprise when it ends in a mere week or two. Maybe your web series was supposed to launch in August, but here it is November, and you're not even done scripting yet.

It's tempting to hide your mistakes behind smoke and mirrors. It's better, though, to abandon this kind of old-media PR spin and just be honest when things don't go the way you'd planned. Audiences are increasingly savvy these days, and a sincere apology and explanation can go a long way. But trying to cover up a mistake by never admitting any fault—that's a great way to burn through a lot of goodwill. Your audience sees right through it. And its members will think the less of you for being dishonest with them.

It all comes down to respecting your audience's time and intelligence. This is one of the underlying reasons it's so very important to make sure that the balance of challenges and rewards in your project is appropriate; if your interactive component is requiring time and travel, you need to make sure that the content earned has an equivalent value, just as much as you'd want to make sure that a film is worth the price of admission.

MODERATION AND GAMEJACKING

Some projects will attract the interest of already-existing communities; others will build a new community from the ground up. No matter where your players gather, though, you'll need to establish how to handle trolls, technical support, and players who break the fourth wall.

Trolls are people who delight in ruining the experience for other people, typically because they think it's fun to do so. If you incorporate any communication or social media elements, you're going to need to develop a policy on how to handle the many kinds of bad behavior you'll see, from the top-tier stuff like offensive or abusive comments, threats of violence, and spam on down to more innocuous behaviors like promoting their own websites, posting inappropriate spoilers, or breaking the fourth wall and talking to your characters as though they aren't real.

If you don't own the platform, there's often not a lot you can do about trolls, beyond flagging or reporting the culprit. The best thing to do with trolls that are outside of your direct reach is just that: flag them and then ignore them. Don't under any circumstances allow yourself to get drawn into an argument. Engaging with trolls is giving them what they want.

On your own sites and forums, though, you need to develop a moderation policy and stick to it. I'm a big fan of hard moderation, though tastes vary. If you're vigilant about deleting offensive comments as soon as they're spotted and warning users who engage in borderline behaviors, especially from the inception of a community, then the tone of the posts will grow to reflect what you consider acceptable. And don't be afraid to ban accounts that keep crossing the line—if an individual is causing grief to the community, the community as a whole will be better off without him.

Good moderation is indispensable if you're planning on allowing comments or running a forum. If you don't have the resources to do any moderation, then you absolutely should not include those elements in your structure.

It's also good design practice to make sure that no player is even capable of ruining the experience for anyone else. That can extend beyond community behavior and into the structure of your game.

Ever heard of *gamejacking*? This is a term for an attempt to hijack your transmedia experience, typically by inserting material that you didn't write into your canon. Often this is done through exploiting your mistakes or oversights and (for example) registering a URL or social media account that is implied in your content—but that you didn't think to register yourself.

Cross-linking is your salvation here. If you develop a strong practice of always linking pieces of game content directly to one another, then this becomes akin to a story checksum; the audience can be certain that if your meta-site or the main thrust of your story doesn't reference the new URL, social media profile, or whatever, then it's not legitimate.

Gamejacking can occur even inside your forums and chat rooms, though, if someone registers an account that looks feasibly like it might be official and then behaves as a character from your story. You can wind up with a very confused audience, unsure of what's part of your story and what's just noise fabricated by another audience member. The best way to handle this is before it ever happens: give official accounts some visual sign or naming scheme that denotes their official status, and lock ordinary players out of acquiring that sign or using similar names.

SOCIAL PROOF

A sock puppet is a persona that is under the control of the transmedia narrative's creative team. Typically a sock puppet is intended to look like a genuine player in the community, but in reality it's someone on the production team (or possibly her friends or family) masquerading as an audience member for the purpose of pointing out key pieces of information, or giving those in the audience solutions when they get stuck.

From the production team's perspective, the appeal of sock puppetry is easy to see. If your audience is veering off on a catastrophically wrong track, or if you've painted yourself into a corner with a plot element or puzzle, and you really, really need someone to say or do the exact right thing in the next hour or your whole house of cards will collapse, then just pretending you're a player who's doing the one right thing that needs doing is seductively easy.

But when you do this, you're robbing your audience of agency. The entire point of creating an interactive drama is to provide those in your audience with that feeling of participation—the feeling that what they say and do and think actually

SEEDING

The launch of a transmedia project is a delicate time. You generally want to reach the widest audience, and you want everyone to come away with a great experience. Unfortunately, there are several myths that creators buy into that can seriously damage their reach and keep participation down. The first and biggest is the idea that a transmedia project doesn't need to be marketed, or that transmedia is its own marketing.

Many creators prefer a subtle, organic approach to seeding, putting content into the world and hoping that somebody notices and cares. But there are strong benefits to pulling in traditional advertising and PR techniques. I can't say this enough: transmedia isn't inherently the same thing as marketing, and so it needs to be marketed in its own right . . . just like every other form of entertainment.

That's not to say you can't go subtle, especially in parallel with a more overt marketing push. But if you're going for something more elegant than a press release and an all-out blitz of bought media and downloadable trailers, then there are a number of things you can do to maximize participation.

First, seed your content in interested communities. When you're targeting your marketing efforts, be very specific about who it is that your story will appeal to. And don't say, "It will appeal to everyone," or, worse, "Males 18 to 45." Both of those are cop-outs at best. Really examine your project and find the things in it that will pull an audience in. (And if you can't find anything, consider going back to the drawing board and making something that's a little more sticky.)

Campfire Media is a master at organic seeding with physical objects—for its HBO *True Blood* campaign, for example, it identified its most-interested audience as people who were really into vampires. So when it seeded that project in the wild by sending out vials of a blood-replacement drink for vampires, it did so by first scouring the Internet for communities of vampire fans.

There is a delicate balance here, however. While you do have to look for your project's natural audience, you also have to be careful not to structure your project to cater to one particular community so much that other potential audiences are alienated. If you rely on one audience too heavily by sticking to their familiar subject matter or tropes, or even using the community's terminology or in-jokes, then you risk making the bulk of your transmedia project inaccessible to any potential audience members who aren't a part of that community already.

Even after you've launched, don't stop seeding until your project is winding down. It's common practice for creators of an ongoing transmedia story to market only at launch, thinking that their entire audience will materialize at that point, and then word of mouth will take over. You can't count on this. Structure your project so that it is accessible to newcomers even two or three weeks, months, or years in.

There are also a couple of things you shouldn't do in the name of promoting your project. First, don't stalk anyone. It's absolutely acceptable for you to create social media presences and promote their existence. It's altogether something else to have your project's accounts start following individuals on Twitter or Facebook, or friending them in other communities. Just don't do it. At best, you won't make much of an impression at all; at worst, it's downright creepy. Let the audience come to you, not the other way around.

And finally, use caution with how you approach the press. Bear in mind that you are not owed coverage. An overenthusiastic creator might send several emails to a journalist or blogger, hoping to catch his attention and get press. Worse, a creator might lobby her player base to do so, hoping to create the impression that there is a groundswell of support for a project. If you want positive press coverage, don't make journalists' lives any harder or more annoying by cluttering up their inboxes. Send them a nice, clear press statement talking about what you're doing and why they should be interested in it. If they don't bite, call it a day.

matters. By just giving away the answers, so to speak, you're creating a situation in which you have shut the door on meaningful player involvement. And if the other players ever find out that you've done this, they will positively hate you for fooling them. Those redundancies and plan Bs that you build into your structure shouldn't ever include just pretending to be a player.

There are other uses for sock puppets, though—times and places where a little sock puppetry can even provide a key element of your experience! You can use them to provide social proof.

Social proof is the demonstration that something has been done or thought of before by other people. The need for social proof is why few people like to be the first person to ask a question in class. It's why shows with a laugh track are rated as funnier by test audiences. It's why you have a better chance of finding a job or a date if you have one already.

Social proof is an important thing in a reality-based game. Sometimes the actions that a player is asked to take in the real world (calling a telephone number, picking up a dead drop, playing poker in a cemetery) are kind of scary if the player doesn't know that someone else is doing them, too. So you provide evidence that another human being is doing the same thing first, removing a huge psychological barrier to allowing your audience to relax and participate.

This is why so many games try to get players to blog, shoot videos, or take photos of their participation. You're creating social proof of involvement, which in turn makes it easier for other players to become involved as well.

If social proof is good and sock puppetry is bad, you might wonder where the line is between these two behaviors. This is the key question to ask yourself: are you opening doors for further participation by your players, or are you closing them? Social proof means showing the players how to do something so that they can do it, too; sock puppetry is showing them how to do it so that they don't have to.

Q&A: MIKE MONELLO

Mike Monello was a producer for *The Blair Witch Project*, and today is a cofounder of Campfire Media, which has executed innovative and award-winning projects for clients like HBO and Discovery. Campfire was *OMMA Magazine*'s small agency of the year for 2011.

Q: *How did you get into transmedia?*

A: It came naturally while we were making *The Blair Witch Project* and reacting to certain opportunities. We were basically five film guys who were lucky enough to have also been exposed to the Internet while in school.

Q: *Can you tell me a little about your favorite projects?*

A: The first one is always the most special, so for me *The Blair Witch Project* was an incredible experience. First, I was working on it with good friends I had met in film school. Second, it was a true indie project, which meant we were free to do whatever we wanted, and that freedom mixed with a lack of resources (that is, money) pushed us into surprising areas that were exciting and new. Finally, it made such a huge splash that it opened the doors for the kind of work we do at Campfire. As for the others, my favorite is always the most recent because it's usually taking everything you've learned previously and pushing it in new directions.

Q: *Where do you see the art and business of storytelling headed over the next few years?*

A: I think it will continue as it always has, with new, usually independent artists pushing the boundaries and seeing their successes slowly co-opted into the mainstream by major companies. I don't believe in all this yammering about

seismic shifts and total transformations. Everything is always changing, too quickly for those making huge profits today and too slowly for those excited by exploring the edges.

Q: *What would you recommend that transmedia creators learn about to improve their craft?*
A: Learn how to build an exceptional team, and learn how to create a culture within the project or company that allows them to do the best work of their lives. Know your strengths, know your weaknesses, and surround yourself with people who are strong where you are weak and vice versa. Then get to work!

Q: *Campfire's seeding when a new project launches is exceptional. What's your approach?*
A: The most important principle here is not to make something cool to give away or send out, but to make something that empowers those who receive it to tell your story. You have to put yourself in their shoes and ask yourself, "If I received this thing, what story would it allow me to tell, and is *that* story interesting to my readers/viewers/listeners/etc?" In other words, you think about both the people you are sending something to and the people that person reaches. In advertising, this is called "propagation planning," and you can find out more about it at Griffin Farley's fantastic site dedicated to the practice: http://griffinfarley.typepad.com/.

Q: *How do you decide which individuals to reach out to?*
A: Early seeding and outreach are usually targeted to specific fan communities, depending on the property or the genre, so we look for people within those communities who are themselves media and content creators. These are the people who are already telling stories and who are more likely to be appreciative of a great outreach piece and more likely to use it to help spread your story.

Q: *What kind of marketing support does a transmedia story need—is word of mouth enough?*

A: Word of mouth is something you earn, you can't pay for it, so there are a lot of factors involved in determining whether you need marketing or media support. If you are creating a transmedia story using IP that is incredibly well known, say a major sci-fi franchise or comic book, then the fan base may be large enough that you can build word of mouth. If you are creating something brand new, you may need marketing support to help get it in front of people. I like to say that a transmedia story architecture should sustain itself and inspire and support word of mouth, but that media or marketing support can act as fuel to make the fire spread faster.

PRODUCTION

17

Project Management:
The Unsung Necessity

Producing a transmedia project can feel a lot like planning a wedding and shooting a feature film at the same time—it requires juggling multiple skill sets and a keen sense of organization. That's because any one project may integrate components from film, event planning, theater, tech development, and more into a single work.

At first, the challenge of pulling all of these pieces together can seem intimidating, even outright impossible. The secret to success: great planning and superb organization.

Ideas are cheap; execution is what separates the dreamers from the doers. The success or failure of a project is determined by its budgets, schedules, task lists, and flowcharts as much as by its creative content.

BUDGETING

You may wonder how much it costs to produce a transmedia story. This is a difficult question to answer, one that's akin to, "How long is a piece of string?" Well, which piece of string are you talking about, exactly?

Transmedia projects can cost millions of dollars to produce (billions, if you include West Coast transmedia projects), or they can be strung together with entirely free resources on volunteer time. The majority of projects will fall somewhere in the middle. But that doesn't help you much when it comes to making a budget.

There are two basic ways to scope out a budget. Either you can envision the project you'd like to make and then work out how much it's going to cost you, or you can work out how much budget you have, and then allocate it to build the best possible project you can. In practice, the budgeting process takes a little bit from both sides—you think up a mechanic and write a proposal for what you'd like the project to look like that you think is in the ballpark in terms of the budget you're expecting, you price it out, and then you add or remove elements (usually it's removing) until your budget and your spec are in line.

As with every kind of budgeting, the cost of a transmedia project can expand to eat up however much budget you give to it, and then some. Don't spend to your last penny; instead, pad your cost estimates as much as you dare, and then pad them some more. It's better to have a reserve to draw on in an emergency than to run out of cash with your project only half completed.

In general, video and technical elements are the most expensive to create; websites and social media can be close to free. You should conceive of a structure that relies most heavily on the media you can afford.

Even no-budget projects have their costs, however. A transmedia project with zero budget is still relying on tools and time spent. You might enjoy spending time honing your craft on a personal project that fires you up as a labor of love. A business, though, would more likely be using labor from employees whose salaries would have to be paid anyway, and repurposing company resources for which money has already been spent—websites on the hosting provider that the company has a relationship with already, for example.

Before you begin a project with a very low budget, you should take stock of the resources you already have on hand, like computers and software; cameras; spaces to work, rehearse, or record; even friends with skills that might be helpful and who might readily do you a favor. If you happen to have a friend who has a talent for creating gorgeous calligraphy, it's worth a few minutes of thought to see whether a gorgeously calligraphed letter might fit into your story (sent out as a real-world artifact, used as a prop in video content, or used as art on a website, for example).

You also have to budget time, not just money. The first step in this is asking everyone on your team how long they think it will take to complete their own contributions. Some project managers will suggest that you then double or even triple all of your initial time estimates to come close to the true time the project will take.

ORGANIZATION

A great story bible is just one element—transmedia projects tend to be incredibly complex and require diligent attention to organization. Project management can make or break you, and a well-organized producer is worth her weight in gold. If you're going to be managing the production yourself, here are a few tools you can use to make the process a little less painful:

1. A complete specification document. Write out exactly what the plan for each medium is, and how each piece is meant to interact with each of the others. This is only a plan for battle, and the plan will inevitably evolve over time. Do your very best to make this spec a living document that is updated as your schedule progresses to keep the whole team (or several teams) on the same page.

2. A spreadsheet with multiple tabs detailing all your assets and pertinent information about them. You need to have a central repository for all login

credentials you might be using on social media or other services, all URLs you have registered, filenames and locations for all photo and video assets, and emergency contact information for every member of your team.

3. A schedule detailing what your deadline is and what milestones you need to hit on your way to that deadline. If you don't have a solid schedule and a meaningful deadline, you'll make very slow progress.

4. A system for communicating project-critical information to your team and archiving particularly important information. Basecamp is currently the standard, but there are alternatives available; Flow, for example, is also a great tool. This might be overkill for a very small team, but the more you scale up, the more crucial it is to track what tasks everyone has on his plate, what's coming up on the calendar, and details about any fires that need putting out.

5. An initial budget, plus an accounting system tracking where all of your money is being spent. (This can also be a simple spreadsheet.) It should keep track of every expense incurred on behalf of the production, from materials to rent to pay for the hours worked by each team member.

6. A safe repository for all your project content that everyone can access—preferably one with a backup system. You can share a drive on a server or use a cloud service like Dropbox. No matter how small your project is, you absolutely must not overlook this.

QUALITY CONTROL

Sloppy work makes you look bad and undermines the integrity of your whole story. It is therefore crucial that you check your work at every turn and on every level. One last double-check never hurts—but one little problem can make you look really bad.

First, make sure that your spelling and grammar are correct. If there are typos, abbreviations, slang, or grammatical errors of any type, make sure you're including them on purpose to demonstrate character. If they serve no deliberate purpose, root them out.

This simple step can reap huge rewards; you only get one chance to make a first impression, after all, and an egregious typo can make just as bad a first impression as bad breath and unlaundered gym clothes would on a first date.

If you're using puzzles or codes, work through the solutions at least twice before you send them out into the world. If possible, you should test your puzzles on someone who wasn't involved in the development process to make sure there is a clear and reproducible answer. You'd be amazed at how players can arrive at an answer to your puzzle that is simpler and more elegant than the one you devised—and how angry they get when that answer doesn't match up with what you had in mind.

If you're using new technology, test it exhaustively under as many different circumstances as you can. Try to get users who weren't in on your development process to try it, too, to make sure that your interface is clear to new users.

If you have a registration process, walk through it from multiple computers. Make sure to try every authentication method you're offering. Make sure your sites look good on at least the most common platforms and web browsers.

If you're running any sort of live or interactive event, do at least one rehearsal to make sure you have everything you need—and everything the players will need, as well. Several rehearsals are even better. I've had the misfortune of being on the team for a live event, only to discover at the last minute that a key piece of infrastructure wasn't in place (like an unexpected lack of wireless service at a venue). Do these rehearsals well before the actual event, as particularly devoted players have been known to show up quite early to scout the scene in case there is some advantage to be gained through familiarity.

There are certainly other measures you can take to ensure the quality of your final project. Think hard about what they are, and then do them. Nothing will break your heart like a small oversight ruining a project you've spent months or years on. Don't take that risk.

METRICS

We all want our project to be a big success, right? But what is "success" exactly?

It isn't the same thing for every project. To be sure, a hundred million audience members and half a billion dollars in revenue would make any project successful by anyone's definition. And yet that's not exactly an attainable goal for every transmedia creator out there. So what is?

Before you can decide whether your project has been successful (or an invaluable learning experience), you need to know exactly why you're making your transmedia story. Are you after money? Press attention? More subscribers for your email list? Brand engagement?

Decide what your concrete goals are even before you begin the project, and the more specific they are, the better. "Brand engagement" isn't a great goal, because there's no way to measure when you've reached it. Fifty thousand likes on your Facebook page, though, or ten thousand Twitter followers, or a hundred thousand plays of your minigame are objective goals that you can track.

Keeping those specific and number-focused goals in mind during design can even be helpful in structuring how your story works. If your goal is to get your audience to sign up for a mailing list, then you're going to need to find a way to make that action appealing in your story. Create a story world method for players to give your their email addresses, and make sure they know you'll be delivering story content through that medium.

But more than knowing what you want, you also need to decide how much you can realistically get. Ideally, you could obtain some benchmarks by looking at numbers for other, similar projects. This information is hard to come by, though Dr. Christy Dena's ARG Stats page (Google it!) is a fantastic start.

One word of warning, though. Some of the numbers for transmedia projects that are out there are presented with a little extra padding and a whole lot of rosy goggles on. Sometimes they're skewed by presenting a number that just doesn't have anything to do with the goals of a project; think of the case where a project shows you how many page views its main site received, but it doesn't tell you how many unique viewers that was, or how many people went on to register. If a site gets ten million page views, but only a thousand people register an account, is that still a success? You'll never be sure if you didn't have a target in mind from the start.

18

Finding and Keeping a Strong Core Team

*T*ransmedia work is very rarely a solo effort. If you want to make a truly multiplatform project, you're probably going to need to build a team.

At a minimum, your project needs people with four distinct skill sets: someone to manage the storytelling, the look and feel, the technology you're using, and the administrative work for the project itself. Sometimes you'll find that these skill sets happily overlap, and that your writer (for example) can manage the whole project. Other times, you'll find that you need multiple people to fill a certain role—for example, the people in charge of the look of your project might be an illustrator plus a web designer, or both of those and also a whole crew of set dressers, costumers, and location scouts.

I'm using "technologist" here as a sweeping category. You might just need somebody who understands tech in a general sense and can put up a website for you, or you might need an actual programmer (or a team of them). A transmedia project that has no technology needs at all is unusual, but if yours are modest, then sometimes your designer or producer can fill that role.

If you're planning to use several media that you aren't experienced with yourself, it's extremely helpful to have someone on your team who is a specialist in each medium you're planning to use. You can always acquire these skills with money (paying a production company to shoot video for you, for example) rather than recruiting these people to your core team. But I find it's vastly superior to integrate as many of these skills as you can into your core creative team. Otherwise, vast quantities of detail that could be used as fuel to further your story will instead be the result of default design decisions, made arbitrarily because the person making them simply didn't know the big picture.

RECRUITMENT

Once you've identified the skills you need, how you find your team members will depend enormously on who you are, how much money you have, and what it is you're making.

Cash-flush enterprises can hire traditional recruiters. Thus far, there's no such thing as a recruiter specializing in transmedia placement, though, so you're probably going to need to weed through a number of candidates who might be excellent at one medium, but don't have the facility for cross-platform and integrated thinking that you require.

Transmedia is often the domain of generalists and bootstrappers, people who are comfortable stepping outside of their job description in order to do whatever needs doing. Bear this in mind when you're recruiting; a great candidate for your project might not be passed on to you by a recruiter who doesn't understand your requirements very well.

It's better to try to identify experienced or even new creators whose existing work is in line with the project you have in mind, and then reach out to them directly.

Even if they're not available for hire, they can often recommend other creators in the same community who will get what you're doing.

For smaller teams that are just starting out, I recommend scouring online and physical communities for kindred spirits. The meetups in New York, Los Angeles, London, Toronto, Vancouver, and a growing number of other cities are a great way of meeting enthusiastic collaborators. Beginners can barter skills, working on each other's projects for mutual gain.

But be careful about what you're asking your collaborators to do, and what its value to them is going to be. I've been approached many times by someone who wanted me to work on his project for free, in return for nothing but credit. There's definitely a place for this kind of thing, but it's at the beginning of your career when you need to establish a solid portfolio. But you can't expect someone to work on just your idea for free and not get anything out of it.

Projects that aim to make money should especially never rely on free or volunteer labor. If you're not valuing your contributors' time with money, you might not be able to count on them to push aside their day jobs or personal projects in order to work on your stuff. Sometimes you get what you pay for.

COMMUNICATION

Transmedia teams work best when there are lots of lines of communication. A traditional production hierarchy might have a chain of command, with everyone reporting to someone above them. Everything is controlled by the person at the top—be that a director, creative director, or publisher.

But transmedia projects tend to be much more complicated and involve very many more moving pieces than a single-media production does, and it's possible that what seems to be a minuscule decision made by someone working in one medium might directly conflict with the same decision made in a different way somewhere else.

Let's say that a writer for the graphic novel drew a panel of Sadie spitting out watermelon in disgust; "I hate watermelon!" she says. But in the film, a set piece involves our hero Sadie fondly remembering the watermelon-and-feta salad she had on a hot afternoon by the seashore. These kinds of factual discrepancies aren't always a big deal, but the observant fan will notice them and think the less of you for them. Missing these things is sloppy.

In a sequential transmedia production, it's imperative that every team be intimately familiar with the work that has gone before and, if possible, be kept in the loop regarding work in progress in other branches of the project. In a spiderweb transmedia production, where multiple pieces are in production and shipping at the same time, it is absolutely key for the teams to be in constant communication.

In nimbler projects, these meetings should be held as often as every day, and major assets should be shared with everyone: scripts, concept art, dailies, prototypes. You can't expect a project to feel like one cohesive piece if it's being produced in silos that never speak to one another.

For bigger, slower-moving projects, it's a good plan to have at least weekly all-staff meetings in which everyone shares progress and assets with the whole team.

As an ongoing practice, different teams should be accessible to one another as much as possible. No component should be an island. Give the web team a way to acquire assets from the film set; make sure the copy for the graphic novel is accessible to the social media crew. If you maximize internal communication, and if you can foster the feeling that separate teams are in collaboration and not competition with one another, the whole story will be stronger for it.

SMALL AND INDIE TEAMS

If you're part of a small team working on a start-up or creating a portfolio piece together, I would especially urge you to create a clear hierarchy of ownership over the project and its timeline. You need to have one person with the uncontested right to make decisions.

Many a hobbyist or grassroots transmedia project has foundered and failed because there was a lack of core accountability inside the team. If nobody has the authority to set a deadline, then nobody is responsible for meeting a deadline, either.

If you aren't paying your team members in money, you have to pay them in credit, at the very least—but you're also going to have to give up some measure of control. Let your team members have some creative authority, even if the genesis of the project is all yours.

This brings in a new problem: when the team members aren't working toward a single creative vision, they might run into problems with conflict resolution. It might not be that one person gets the final say in every category, but maybe your writer should get final decision-making power on story matters, the visual designer should get final say on which color to use, and so on. Work out who has the final say over what area ahead of time. If you wait for a conflict to arise, then even deciding how conflict resolution should work will be fraught with tension.

That's not to say that collaboration among equals can't work. Some of the most personally and professionally rewarding years of my life have been spent working with collaborators in a democratized setting. But the sort of trust that arrangement requires is built over months of experience at actually working together, hitting deadlines, and crafting something together that you're all proud of. It's possible to fall into a situation like that even among a group of volunteers . . . but it's exceedingly rare.

I don't mean that the project owner should turn a deaf ear to any input from teammates, however. That, too, is a recipe for unhappy collaborators, and ultimately a failed project. Every person on your team deserves the right to help shape your story.

And if there is any chance of money on the table derived from your work, you're going to need to be very clear about how it will be divided. You also need to really, really trust the people you work with—but you need your agreement in writing, too. Choosing a business partner is as big a commitment as getting married. In both cases, if you make a bad choice, you can get cleaned out and left bleeding. Get a prenup, kids. The love might not last forever, but a signed contract does.

OUTSOURCING TRANSMEDIA

Not everyone who picks up this book will be a creator in the trenches. Instead, you may be in a position to hire a team to build out a project on your behalf. Let's say you're working at an entertainment company—a movie studio, say, or a TV network; or maybe you're with a company offering a consumer product or service, and your agency is encouraging you to explore transmedia techniques in order to extend your brand. You're an interested party. But you don't have the time (or perhaps the skills) to execute the project on your own.

Sometimes, the right thing to do is to pass the baton: hire a specialty production company, a small agency, or even a handful of freelancers to build the project for you.

This can be a very frustrating position, because you still want to produce great work, but you may not have much direct creative influence over the project—and you may not have a lot of control over the corporate policies the project has to conform to, either. But make no mistake, the role of the commissioner or client-side account manager has tremendous influence over the shape and success of the project.

Here are a few things you should do to ensure that you get the best work out of your transmedia consulting team—and don't get in its way.

1. Get internal buy-in. If you're part of an ad agency or a marketing department, the most important thing you need is buy-in for the project from the top decision maker or visionary. That could be the client, the CEO, or, in the case of entertainment marketing, the filmmaker or showrunner. These are the people who can stop your project in its tracks by withholding an approval. They can also completely derail your project by asking for changes without realizing that there can be a cascade of implications that ultimately destroy the whole project's structural integrity. It's your job to make sure that the key stakeholder knows what your team is doing, and is excited about it.

2. Be up-front about your corporate limitations—moderation policies, social media policies, and so on. It is a creator's worst nightmare to start building out a project, only to learn at the eleventh hour that the whole structure has to be reworked because (for example) it uses individualized responses to Twitter as a key technology, but you're forbidden to tweet to individual users from any corporate account.

   If possible, you should be proactive about seeking out those boundaries. Bring in your lawyers and policy makers early in the project, ideally during the development of the concept. If you wait to run a finished proposal by your legal team for sign-off, you're practically begging for a very nasty surprise should one of the key mechanics your entire project is built on wind up being vetoed.

3. Cut yourself out as a middleman as much as possible. Waiting for you to act as a go-between for your legal team or internal tech department, for example, can slow things down and ultimately kill your project, particularly if it has a heavily responsive interactive piece. It's fine to insist that you remain in the loop (in fact, it's only sensible), but it's counterproductive not to let the different resources of your whole project communicate directly.

4. Don't go rogue. Every now and again, I've seen a transmedia client slip something into a project without the team of core creators knowing about it ahead of time. If you unwittingly change a major plot point or accidentally remove a key clue to solving a challenge, this can make your whole house of cards fall down. Tell the team members what you want to have happen, and then let them do it. It's their job to figure out how to get the desired result.

5. Give your transmedia team the keys to your social media platforms, or make sure that the people who have those keys are available day and night. If an emergency arises outside of regular business hours, every second that you don't officially respond makes it just a little worse. Make sure your team has the tools to put out a fire fast.

6. Make sure you know exactly what the plan is. If you don't thoroughly understand what the plan is and why it's structured the way it is, ask questions until you do understand. Don't make any assumptions. The potential for a miscommunication to have very unpleasant implications down the road is high, particularly if something in the plan is against company policy.

7. Don't panic at the first sign of criticism. Some people are going to hate your project, and there is nothing you can do about it. Take a deep breath and repeat that to yourself a few times. That means that if you get any sizable audience to speak of, you'll inevitably see forum posts and tweets talking about how much you suck when you first launch, and again every time you introduce a new element or piece of content. This is OK. You can't please all the people all the time. Tamp down on the panic moving you to change around the entire structure of your project to please one or two vocal critics.

   That said, there is a time and a place for changing your project to respond to criticism. Sometimes the haters have it right, and sometimes you and your designers will be better off adapting on the fly. But such a response should be measured, calm, and carefully thought through. At the very least, make sure you're reacting because of a widely held opinion, not just one squeaky wheel.

8. If you don't trust your team and its professional judgment, hire someone else. There may come a point when you're not sure whether something is going to work or not. If you've hired a good team, you should be comfortable accepting its judgment on challenge design, audience management, and so on. If you can't trust the people on the team you've hired to know what they're talking about, you're better off working with someone else.

19

Websites and Tech Development: DIY or Outsource?

*E*very transmedia project will have at least one website somewhere. Aside from the basic landing page with information about a project, web content commonly includes blogs and microsites that exist within the fictional universe.

But if you haven't ever created a website before, then all of the little steps that go into it can be quite intimidating. You have to buy a domain name, find hosting, get a good-looking design, worry about security, prevent comment spammers, and learn to use metadata. It's a lot to handle.

But just as you don't need to make a full-blown nine-platform transmedia project all in one shot, you don't need to become a technical guru just to put up a website. You can avoid a lot of complexity by just using someone else's service (Tumblr, WordPress, Squarespace, and the like). It's more professional-looking to own your own space, though.

First, the bare basics. A domain name is what people type into their web browser to get to your site. Google.com is a domain name, for example; so are Amazon.com and Zombo.com. You're likely to want your very own domain name for your sites.

Pick something snappy that fits your story, something that's easy to remember and easy to spell. Don't get too attached to your first idea for a domain name. It's a good bet that most of the ones you'll think of have already been taken by someone else.

The next step is registering your chosen domain name online. There are many registrars out there that can do this for you; popular ones include GoDaddy, Network Solutions, Dice, Joker, and Pair. If you want to break out of the standard .com and .org mold, you may need to go to one specific registrar. Many of these top-level domains (as they're called) represent and are managed by one particular country. National top-level domains don't always allow just anyone to register—many of them require a valid business presence in that country.

Be absolutely sure that you never link to, hint at, or outright state a domain name or a social media account name before you've actually registered it. If you haven't done this, it's highly likely that someone else will swoop in and register it for you—and you won't be able to count on his good nature, either. Some projects' launches have been completely skewered by this simple oversight.

Buying a domain name is cheap, though it is also a recurring annual cost. Watch out for expensive and unnecessary add-ons for services you might not need. One common offer that's worth taking a second look at is private registration. When you register a domain name, you are required to provide contact information for technical and administrative reasons. A clever audience member can and will take a look at that information to test the edges of your story world. If you're not comfortable having your personal or business contact information publicly available, you should pay for a private domain registration service.

If your domain registration is in the name of a character, then the emails and phone numbers in the whois had better be functional. The kinds of audiences that would be inclined to look at that information in the first place will expect a payoff for their efforts.

The next thing to sort out is hosting. Your domain name is something like a street address, so that people know where to find you on the Internet. But that doesn't give you a working website just yet, just like having a lot on a street doesn't mean there's a house there. Your website needs to live on a web server for other people to get to it; that's called a host. DreamHost, Laughing Squid, and Media Temple all have great reputations. If you expect a very heavy volume, though, you should look into a balance-loading host like Amazon Web Services—and hire dedicated technical staff to manage it for you.

DESIGN

Web design is a skill and art that is often undervalued. I highly advocate paying for the services of a web designer; it's a budget line item that's well worth it, since the polish of your web presence will have a huge impact on what people think of you and your project. A truly talented web designer with experience in transmedia will also be able to help you find opportunities to extend the storytelling into your visuals by choosing fonts, colors, and layouts that underline your worldbuilding and characterization efforts.

If you can't afford a web designer, you might be tempted to try to design your site on your own. Unless you are yourself an experienced web designer, I don't recommend this. The tools are readily available, but design is a skill that must be honed. Don't let first impressions of your whole project go sour just to save a little money.

A good middle ground would be to build your site on a common platform and search for predesigned themes. The popular platform right now is WordPress. While it is blogging software, it's customizable enough that it's also commonly used for all kinds of websites. A quick search on the web for "WordPress themes" will give you a treasure trove of options, mostly professionally designed, for much less

money than a custom design would run you. You can choose the ones you like and install them with just a few clicks. Many WordPress themes even include customization options so that you can tweak colors, fonts, and layout on your own.

If you do hire a professional web designer, though, one of the most important things you can do is clue her in on the big picture. I like to involve a designer on a higher level than simply handing down a very specific wireframe and a completely finished functional spec; after all, I'm not the artist with the best skill set for making those decisions. But it can also be frustrating for the designer to hear nothing more specific than, "OK, go make a website for a fake bank."

Most work will fall somewhere in between these two extremes. Here are a few things you and your web designer should consider when designing a site:

1. **Realism.** Often, the website you're designing will have real-world analogues. If you're making a fictitious site for a church, find some church websites to look at. If you're making a website for a megalithic industrial company, take a look at the design for companies like Boeing or Lockheed Martin. You won't want to copy these sites wholesale, but you'll get design cues from existing sites that can give your work a little more verisimilitude.

2. **Content length.** Before you create an initial design, make sure to have a discussion with the interaction designer or writer regarding how much copy he expects to write for the site (and therefore how much space you'll need to allow for it). Instead of just knowing that there will be "news," for example, you need to be on the same page about creating short news bullet points or page-long press releases; and if you need a section for a thousand-word treatise on the corporate mission, you'll want the designer to know this up front.

3. **Space for any multimedia elements.** Make sure you know what kinds of media will be integrated into every site, be that video, audio, or a stream from a social media widget. If the project requires these elements, you'll

need to provide a place for them on your website. You don't want to design a sleek, tight website for a finance company and find at the last second that you have nowhere to embed the CEO's climactic resignation speech.

There are also a few things you shouldn't include in a web design unless you have a specific purpose in mind for them.

1. **Locations and/or maps.** Don't ever put addresses or maps in a design unless they are relevant to your story. Many transmedia experiences extend into the real world, and there isn't a good way to indicate that yours won't, short of leaving out location information entirely. Never, never give your fictitious company a real-world address . . . unless you actually want somebody to turn up and knock on that door.

2. **News sections.** Particularly for a long-running game spanning dozens of websites, a news section is a pernicious creature. News must be updated periodically to maintain the illusion of a living and persistent story world. If all of your one-off corporate websites have news sections, you may soon get bogged down by the obligation to come up with side content for them at the expense of your core story.

3. **Login forms.** That blank user/password entry area is a signal to players that at some point, they will be able to get access to something more. If this doesn't happen, your audience will feel frustrated at the red herring. Don't put in login forms merely as a design element.

These are just the bare-bones basics. It's enough to get you started for a small-scale project, but there are any number of other things you'll need to be aware of for your web presence, particularly as your potential audience grows.

Luckily, if there's one thing the web is good at, it's teaching you how to use the web better. If you don't have a technical background, but you're still on the hook to manage your web presence, it's a good idea to spend some time researching web

server security, spam prevention, metadata, and search engine optimization. There is a wealth of free information available, if you just take the time to look for it.

TECH DEVELOPMENT

Let's talk about code, baby.

Many projects can be assembled with off-the-shelf technical resources. There are tools from SocialSamba to Storify to HootSuite, Scavengr, Broadcastr, and Wanderlust Stories, all of which can bring unique benefits to your story.

But sometimes you just have to roll your own. Technical development adds a new (and, for many, unfamiliar) layer of concern to a project. You'll need to pay attention to source code versioning, bug tracking, and play-testing across multiple platforms. As with other kinds of specialty media production, if you don't already know how to do technical development, the best thing you can do is locate a skilled technologist to help you, either by hiring one or by finding a collaborator.

With technical development, it's not necessary for the primary creator to learn to code personally, but it helps to have a basic understanding of how the underlying technology works. Sometimes this knowledge can spark ideas for new interactions and uses that would never have occurred to you just from looking at a finished product. So even if you outsource your tech development, try to get some idea of what's going on under the hood.

If you do code your own, version management can be a serious problem for technical development. It's a good idea to use a code repository like Git to handle different versions of your code, particularly if your team has several programmers on it. Otherwise you may find multiple developers working at cross-purposes, with one saving over another's work by mistake.

It's also a good idea to maintain one (or several) development environments, in addition to any audience-facing live servers. That gives you the opportunity to test changes before you push them out into the public eye, to make sure you haven't inadvertently broken something else.

There are a few common rookie technical mistakes you can make, particularly with web content, which you should particularly be on the lookout for.

1. **Predictable or story-breaking naming and foldering schemes.** Don't use folder or file names that are predictable—especially not if you're rolling out that content over a long period of time. Players have been known to do speculative searching, so if you have an image named ponies1 on your server, someone is going to look and see whether ponies2 and ponies3 exist, too. It's a good idea not to make the folders of your web server browsable at all, so that your audience can't go exploring for content you're not ready to release yet (or worse, content you never meant to release at all.)

   You also won't want to mention anything you don't want players to look at in a robots.txt file. Players aren't robots, and they will be curious to see what it is you don't want robots to look at. Just keep it offline until it's time.

2. **Putting up a solvable puzzle, but not the reward content behind it.** This one can be problematic on several levels. The common example is the username/password combination that starts working only after it's been up for several hours, days, or weeks. The problem? Your audience may have tried the correct combination early on and concluded, when it didn't work, that it wasn't correct—and they may never try the right thing again. Frustration city.

   For other kinds of puzzles (leading to new URLs, for example, or to other specific pieces of content that simply aren't up yet), if the reward isn't there, the players either will erroneously assume they're wrong and keep working, or will feel cheated that they jumped through your hoop and didn't get a treat out of it. Neither one is good news for your project. You can't let players' work go unrewarded and expect to maintain an enthusiastic audience.

   You may think that you have a few hours or days of grace time, and that there is absolutely no way anyone would get there before you've put up the reward or linked content. You're almost certainly wrong. But either way, do you really want to bet your whole project on it?

3. **Letting your slip show.** This category includes letting your audience see story world-breaking foldering schemes (for example, /www/clients/warnerbrothers/approved). It might include commented-out links to sites you don't want discovered yet, or notes to other developers on the team (or to yourself). You'll want to scrub images, audio, and other documents of metadata mentioning the names of the writers, business names, or location tags that don't fit into your fiction. Among some audiences, looking at source code—even decompiling Flash files to see if anything is hidden in them—is a common activity. You'll want yours to be as smooth and clean as a fresh bar of soap. Don't leave anything your players might grab onto . . . unless it's there on purpose.

Q&A: ADRIAN HON

Adrian Hon is the chief creative officer and cofounder of the award-winning studio Six to Start, which has produced *We Tell Stories*, *Smokescreen*, and *The Code*. He has recently released the runaway Kickstarter success *Zombies, Run!*

Q: *How did you get into transmedia?*

A: My first introduction was through *The Beast*, the ARG for the movie *A.I.*; I was one of the moderators of the player community (the Cloudmakers), and the game really struck a chord with me. While I was pursuing a degree in neuroscience at the time, I started up a blog about ARGs, and in 2004 I joined Mind Candy to become the executive producer and lead designer of the *Perplex City* ARG. In 2007 I left to set up Six to Start with my brother, Dan.

Q: *Where do you see the art and business of storytelling headed over the next few years?*

A: I think we'll start seeing more stable formats emerge. At the moment, there's a massive amount of experimentation going on, which is great, but it also means that we haven't found anything that works reliably and is profitable. We don't have the equivalent of an app or a book or an hour-long TV episode yet, but when we do, life will be a lot easier, and we'll be able to focus our innovations and creativity in a better way.

From a technological point of view, we'll see transmedia projects become even simpler to navigate, especially across a range of devices, from phones to tablets to computers.

Q: *What would you recommend that transmedia creators learn about to improve their craft?*

A: I'd suggest both sampling as many transmedia experiences as possible (even just trying the first 10 minutes is fine) and trying to make your own. It is absolutely essential that you try to make your own—that's the only way you'll have a proper appreciation of what skills and tasks are involved in production, and how tricky some things can be!

Q: *Six to Start has a reputation for using novel technologies as storytelling platforms. Can you talk a little about your approach to using new tech?*

A: We're actually quite reluctant to use the most cutting-edge tech, because it's often very limited in terms of potential audience and it can be so finicky to deal with that you don't have as much energy to dedicate to the other creative parts of the project. New tech is great for marketing and for demos, but not so good for products that need to reach massive numbers of people or make money.

Instead, our approach is to use new tech *immediately after* it has become easier to develop for and has proper tools. For example, it used to be quite time-consuming to run interactive voice response phone lines or to do iPhone development; now, tools are available that simplify both processes tremendously. Likewise, in a year or two, it will be much easier to do augmented reality development on smartphones, and we'll start looking at that as well.

Q: What advice would you offer a creator who wants to include a tech-heavy element, but doesn't have much technical background?

A: You really have two options. The first is to learn the technology yourself. That's not quite as silly as it sounds because there are some fantastic tutorials (and even games) out now that will teach you how to do some pretty impressive stuff, and of course, knowing how to program is a skill that will pay dividends for years.

But let's assume you can't do that—that means you'll need to find a partner who can do the tech for you. Contrary to popular belief, it is not easy to simply find a developer and convince them to work on your amazing idea for free in return for a piece of the action; not only are good developers highly sought after, but they also have their own creative ideas that they can pursue on their own. So consider doing the reverse: find developers who are already interested in making transmedia projects and offer your help and assistance in design and writing. That's a great way to build up experience and trust, and to establish good relationships that you can take further.

Q: How much of a technical background do you think is necessary to be a transmedia creator?

A: It's important to understand the tools that you use, even if you don't necessarily use them yourself. Good film directors will know the capabilities of their cameras and lighting, and will know roughly how easy or difficult it is to do certain scenes in CGI, even if they've never been a cameraman or lighting technician or visual effects artist themselves. Likewise, at the very least, you need to understand the strengths and weaknesses of the different tools you want to use, and how difficult it is to use them. There's no quicker route to frustration than wanting to implement a difficult piece of technology, but thinking that it'll be easy—or vice versa!

20 Don't Be a Jerk on Social Media

*U*sing social media seems like a no-brainer in today's highly connected environment. But the whats and hows vary tremendously from project to project, and some formerly common uses are falling into disrepute.

In our bootstrapping grassroots history, it was once a common thing to create social media profiles for a fictional character, and have that character behave as though the profile were for a real person. This isn't always as good an idea as it sounds. You have to be very sensitive to the rules and the culture of the platform you plan to use, to make sure that what you're up to isn't going to be considered bad manners (or worse).

For example, Facebook explicitly forbids making a profile for a character. That's right—no matter what else you've seen or read out there, creating a profile for a fictional character is against the Facebook terms of service, and if anybody rats you out, Facebook will close

the profile with no recourse. Projects have been completely derailed by less. The firm's solution is to allow you to make fan pages for those characters; but this can be illusion-breaking.

And then there's the chat issue. As of this writing, it's impossible to permanently log out from Facebook chat, which means that every time a member of your team checks in to post an update, there's the risk that a sharp-eyed player will spot him and send a message. If the person who's logged in doesn't happen to be the writer for that character, this can be a particularly tight spot.

The most recent social media network to launch is Google+. It doesn't have the chat issue that Facebook does, but so far, it's copying Facebook's stance on requiring the real name of each user, not a nickname or a pseudonym. That means that fictional characters aren't welcome there, either, and there's no way to accommodate them to date.

And then there's the problem of LinkedIn. Some games have created character profiles on LinkedIn. Heck, I've done it myself! But as time goes on, I'm less and less enthusiastic about the idea. LinkedIn is inherently a forum for business, not for play, and a user who stumbles on your content through LinkedIn isn't going to be alert for the signs that this isn't for real. People may interact with your fake LinkedIn profile genuinely, falsely hoping that they might get a job, an introduction, or some other career-minded benefit from it.

Especially in these days of rampant unemployment, it seems to me to be particularly cruel to jerk around people who are looking for a job or trying to build a stable career. It's my policy now to stay off LinkedIn, and I'd encourage you to do the same.

So where are fictional characters welcome? Well, there's always Twitter. Twitter has long been a venue for content that isn't meant to be taken with a straight face, from profiles like @bronxzooscobra (a Twitter stream from the point of view of the snake that escaped from the Bronx Zoo in the spring of 2011) to those by dead celebrities (Elvis Presley, George Washington) or religious figures (there must be at least a dozen Jesus Christs alone).

Such Tweet Sorrow, a Twitter adaptation of *Romeo and Juliet*
Image used with permission of Mudlark

The culture of Twitter is very playful, and so many fiction projects using Twitter have flourished. Jay Bushman is a specialist in that, but he's certainly not the only one; Twitter users have staged a complete retelling of Stephen King's *The Stand* over a period of months; performed *War of the Worlds 2.0*, a reenactment of the famous radio drama; and banded together to play as the characters from favorite story worlds such as *Lord of the Rings*, the TV shows *Mad Men* and *Game of Thrones*, and so on.

There's even *Such Tweet Sorrow*, a project using Twitter to retell *Romeo and Juliet*! (And it wasn't me who did it, either.)

Of course, nobody is saying that the only use for social media is to impersonate characters. There is a rich vein of ways to use social media to keep in touch with your audience on a meta level, too, that you can mine—talking about your game in a straightforward way, undisguised by layers of fiction. It's a great idea to use a presence outside of your story to provide technical support and other urgent communications, or to provide news about what to expect from your story next.

Not every project has this out-of-story presence, and as a result, many projects suffer from frustrated players who don't have a fast, easy way to contact the storytellers. You might not need to use this presence much, but if you ever need it in a hurry, you'll need it to be already established as a credible source for story information, so you can't leave it until the last minute.

SHARING MECHANICS

Getting your audience members to act as your recruiters is only common sense nowadays. This is one of the vast benefits of using social media. If there is no way for your audience to share information about your story on Facebook, Twitter, Google+, Tumblr, Pinterest, or whatever else happens to be the trendy network du jour, then you've missed a huge opportunity. You can count on some word of mouth the (relatively) old-fashioned way, by people sending each other links manually in email or through instant messaging . . . but it's going to happen a lot more often if it's as simple as clicking a button.

There is a dark side to sharing, though, that you should be very sensitive to. The modern media landscape is crowded with demands on people's time and attention. Everyone and everything begs you to share. As a result, audiences are increasingly selective. They see right through you. They know perfectly well that they're just being used as a marketing vector. And by and large, they don't like it much.

So your story has to rise above and beyond the media chatter to become something that people actually want to share—it has to give them a reason.

Some designers solve this problem by forcing the player's hand. If you want to unlock the next video or episode in the story, they say, first send out this affiliate link to recruit your friends. Tweet this hashtag to enter your solution to our question.

You must have five (or 10, or 50) friends also playing to get to this level. At first blush, this seems like a fair deal; the players get something they want, and you get something you want, too.

But this approach often backfires. People don't like being forced to share when they don't want to—and sure, some people will share with their friends under these conditions, but a lot won't. Quite a few people will abandon your story entirely once it becomes clear that you're interested in them only as vectors for sharing links. Privacy doesn't matter to everyone, but it really, really matters to the people who do care about it.

That's not to say that you shouldn't provide any incentive for sharing links on social media. Obviously sharing is beneficial to your project, and providing your players with an incentive to share is logical. Just don't make it blackmail. The incentive should be something your audience wants, but don't lock away entire parts of your experience from those who aren't comfortable sharing. Always provide them with another way to get to the same content.

That way can be harder or more time-consuming; that's fine. But you shouldn't go out of your way to alienate users who prefer to keep their activities private. A remarkably large number of early adopters and influencers feel this way. The larger your audience, the more selective you're going to be in what you share, and with whom; you don't often see Twitter users with hundreds of thousands of followers tweeting links to games or contests. And these are the people you want to like you most.

So the right approach is to make sharing advantageous, but not necessary to progress further in your story. It's even better if the advantage is subtle; if you're running a competition, it won't sit well if the biggest number of points to be won is through recruiting friends (unless that's explicitly what your game is about).

And make sure that the things you're asking your audience to share are actually worth sharing. Ideally these would be easy entry points into your story—a rabbit hole. But it's just as good to share tidbits of later material that tease at the mood and plot of the whole. Failbetter Games's *Echo Bazaar* is particularly talented at this. It does lock some content away from players who want a solitary experience, which

Echo Bazaar has exquisitely shareable writing
Image used with permission of Failbetter Games

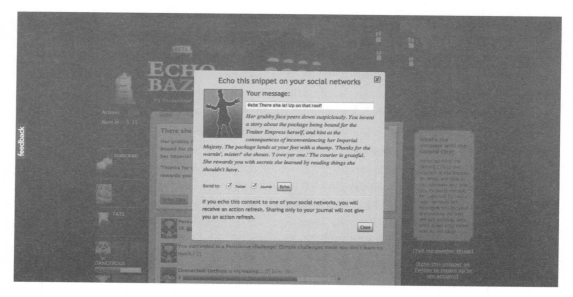

I generally frown upon. But it also provides delicious morsels of copy in the social media messaging it provides for you—something you'd want to share, not something you have to share to keep playing.

It's light-years better than a bald and boring, "I'm playing #somegame. Join my team for 500 points!"

21

Email and Phone: Cheap and Effective

*E*mail can be a real workhorse for transmedia, alerting players to new content or creating the illusion of a personal relationship with a character. This chapter offers guidelines on how to best use a few high-impact emails, and delineates the pros and cons of using free email accounts, how to harvest email addresses in a story-consistent context, and how to avoid coming across like a spammer.

If you plan to use outbound email, the first step is acquiring contact information from your audience. The best possible way to collect email addresses is to have your players give them to you—not buying a list. It's fabulous if you can do this in the guise of participating in the fiction. Past projects have collected email addresses via web forms asking the audience to apply for a job, for example, or to RSVP to a protest rally.

But there's nothing wrong with having a very clear out-of-story place for your players to give you their contact information to be used

in the story. This is another useful purpose for a meta-site, along with cross-linking and rolling story recaps. It's elegant when information such as this can be gathered as part of your fiction, to be sure, but don't let your logistics suffer because you can't find a place to fit it into the story gracefully.

Outbound email can be a rich way to create character interaction or to keep your audience in the loop for new developments in your project, from plot twists to launch dates. There are two basic ways to handle outbound email: you can do one-off personalized responses to inbound mail, or you can craft prewritten bulk emails and send them out all at once. Which method to choose will depend on how much email you expect to receive; it's almost impossible to personalize a very large volume of email.

On the other side of the coin, accepting inbound email for the characters in your story has quite a few potential uses, too. For one thing, you can use it to keep your finger on the pulse of your audience's reactions to your project as it plays out. It can also provide a point of interaction—your story might hinge on somebody emailing you the correct passcode to get into a safe deposit box, for example. But managing an inbox can be a high-volume and low-reward task for your development team. Don't feel obligated to do this, especially not by hand.

There is one way to split the difference between ignoring inbound email and bogging yourself down in responsive writing. You can use autoresponders—these are email messages automatically sent in reply to anyone who sends you an email.

I'm a bit of a curmudgeon about autoresponders; too often these are boring, lifeless pieces of text containing little to nothing of real interest to the reader. Don't let the player's effort of sending an email go unrewarded by sending him a generic, thoughtless autoresponder; take your time and instead craft something that builds character, at the very least, even if it doesn't further your plot.

Better yet, autoresponders can sometimes be configured to fire only in response to an email containing a particular word or phrase. This can be really handy—for example, you could set up an account that would automatically send a response saying, "That was the right code—that safe deposit box contained only this vial of sand. Wonder what it means?"—but only if the received email includes the correct safe-deposit passcode.

EMAIL ACCOUNTS

There are two kinds of email available. You can use free email, or you can use hosted email.

Free email accounts (from services like Gmail and Hotmail) are better for smaller-scale projects and for sending out personalized email responses. The benefit of them is that they're free, which is an important consideration for any project with a lean budget.

They also look pretty convincingly like real people, which can be a bonus for you, depending on the kind of fiction you're trying to spin. And, of course, it's very simple to send emails from these accounts quickly, as long as you're not trying to send to very many people at a time.

One warning: if you're using a consumer-level free email account in your fiction, and you're sending email to more than a single player at a time, be sure to put all of them into the "BCC" field, not the "To" or "CC" field. If you include multiple email addresses in the "To" or "CC" fields, you'll be revealing those players' addresses to one another. This is at best a breach of privacy, and at worst cause for legal action against you.

If you're going to need to send and receive any significant volume of email, though—more than a real person is likely to send—you're going to need hosted email. You'll also need it if you'd like to use a custom email address (for example, romeo@montaguesrock.com). That means that somewhere out there, there is a server handling your email.

Using hosted email addresses means that the part after the @ belongs to you and only you. This has some very significant advantages. For one thing, it creates a much higher barrier to entry for someone who's trying to impersonate one of your characters. (If you use only free resources, it's a lot easier for a gamejacker to insert herself into your story and try to derail it.)

And having your own domain name as part of your email address creates a sense of legitimacy that can be priceless, particularly if some of your email will come from institutions or organizations in your fiction. Which email address feels more like it comes from a credible business to you: biovision-press@aol.com, or press@biovision.com?

BULK EMAIL

From time to time, you may want to send out big batches of emails, either as a promotional tool or as a device to further your story. For example, your fiction might have your talented musician in a position where he's desperate for cash . . . and just then, you send out email to all the members of your audience with a photo of a flyer for a Battle of the Bands (with the prize money conveniently just the amount of money he needs).

For projects with a live piece that rolls out over several weeks, it's an excellent idea to plan on sending your audience a weekly reminder or update email. But don't send email more than once a week unless it's an interactive part of your fiction, or unless the duration of your project will be quite short (say, less than two weeks)—daily messages about new unlocked content will generally feel overwhelming to your audience, and could backfire.

If your project is a slower-moving one, even weekly emails might be too much. For a years-long sequential transmedia franchise, once every two weeks is probably your limit; and remember, since you burn a little bit of goodwill every time you send an email, don't send too many of them just to remind fans that you still exist. Make sure you're telling them something that they genuinely want to know: announcing a release date, for example.

Don't consider your hard-won email list as a vehicle for ads promoting your content (or worse, someone else's). Remember, the list has value to you only as long as the readers feel like you're providing value to them.

If you're sending out email in any significant quantity (and I mean more than a few dozen), I highly recommend subscribing to a bulk email service like MailChimp. MailChimp and similar services will append a footer to your outbound messages and handle list management, so you don't have to deal with stuff like people unsubscribing all by yourself. As a bonus, you'll also get some statistics on how many of your emails bounce and so on.

It's tempting to want to send out in-story emails without all that fiction-breaking stuff in the footer. It's tempting, but it's totally not worth it. If you're sending out bulk emails and you don't provide an option for unsubscribing, then congratulations! You're a spammer!

In the United States, at least, there is very tight regulation of the conditions under which you can send out email—to comply with the CAN-SPAM act, emails must conform to some pretty stringent criteria, including that unsubscribe option and including a physical address for postal mail.

CAN-SPAM technically applies only to commercial messages, but any email sent out as a part of your transmedia experience might be considered commercial in the eyes of the law. And fines for violating these regulations can be as steep as $16,000 for each email sent. That's a lot of money to gamble, if you ask me, especially when your audience is unlikely to actually read a footer anyway. Why take the risk?

If you're part of an organization with a bigger marketing department, you may already have resources to rely on for sending email (and policies to comply with, too). Be sure to check with the appropriate people in your organization well before you need to send any email, while you're still in the planning stages. I've seen organizations that need up to a month just to set up an inbox for an email account; and in some companies, reading and responding to inbound email will be logistically complex, maybe even needing the involvement of your legal advisors.

Then again, I've also seen situations where email and other social media should have been run by a client or legal team before going live, and the project's owner relied on the "Ask forgiveness, not permission" adage. If you can do that, great! If you're risking your job over it, though, make sure it's worth the gamble.

22

Making and Using Prerecorded Content

If you plan to include video in your narrative, very often it will be the central medium around which the rest of your project is structured.

Audio and video can be the most expensive and complicated components of a transmedia production. To record film, you need a whole host of skills: casting, directing, acting, set dressing, costuming, prop manufacturing, lighting, and editing. And you need the equipment to record on, the space to record in, and the logistical skills to make sure that you get everything in place at the right time. Film production has fostered some of the finest producers and project managers I've met across any field.

Because video is expensive to shoot and complex to set up, many projects incorporating video content will shoot it before the project is even launched. It's cheaper and easier by far to shoot 10 three-minute video clips all in one go than it is to try to manage your actors'

and crews' schedules to put together 10 sessions, each aiming at one three-minute video clip.

This is fine when your video components serve as milestones for your overall story to pass through, and you know you won't have to make any changes. A transmedia project grounded in a TV show, for example, will know precisely what those scripts will be, sometimes even months in advance.

Prerecorded audio and video are some of the least flexible media, though. If you want to change a story element as your narrative plays out, reshooting is rarely an option—the actors may have been booked on something else, or it could cost too much money to get the crew together. It might even be that you need to have the video ready to post, air, or distribute in two days, but it would take two weeks or more to gear up.

If that's the case, then you'll need to think about how to work around those immovable set pieces in the story. If making changes at the last minute simply isn't possible, introduce some ambiguity into your prerecorded video so that multiple interpretations can all be valid.

Or go for the brass ring and do a sort of production on the fly, in which you determine in advance that you'll use video content at regular intervals or at planned plot points, but you leave the actual shooting until the last minute—or even do live streaming. This can be a little hair-raising; after all, you're holding your project hostage to the possibility that your lead will get hit by a bus, your location will be flooded out, somebody will tip a vat of grape juice onto your one-of-a-kind irreplaceable prop, and so on.

But if you can do it, the benefit to your project is amazing. Instead of your story being on rails, you can truly be reactive to your audience, so that even video becomes a dialogue, not a monologue. You can even mention specific audience members by name—a thrill to the individual player, but also to the community as a whole because it grounds your story in reality. It tells your audience that you're paying attention.

You can split the difference, of course. It's not all or nothing—you can preshoot lots of video, including a few alternate versions to account for places in your story where you know branching is likely to occur. Then you can either edit the correct versions just before you push them live or put them on the air, or else you can shoot just a little bit of supplemental video and add it to what you had already at the last possible moment.

PRODUCTION

In theory, all you need to produce video content is a video camera and someone to hold it. In practice, though, video production is arguably the most complex component of a transmedia project. You need the camera and someone to hold it, sure, but you also need a suitable place to film, a script for your scene, props in order, actors and costumes, and a producer keeping tabs on everything to make sure every single one of those balls in the air gets caught on the way back down.

If you don't have much of a background in film or audio recording, your very best bet is to find an experienced collaborator (or at least someone with more experience than you). Ideally, you would hire a media production company—preferably one that has worked on transmedia projects before. If your budget just won't permit that, you can try contacting local universities to see if they have a film department; you might be able to persuade a student to work with you.

If you're dead set on DIY, though, do as much research as you can ahead of time on best practices for film. I am by no means an expert on video, audio, or film production, but here are a few practical notes that might help you get a running start.

First, organization is absolutely crucial. You need to be able to track every prop, every scene, every line, and every actor.

Make storyboards ahead of time showing what you want to capture on film. Make sure your performers get their scripts well ahead of time, so that they can rehearse (alone or together, whichever is more suitable for your material). Even if you do, you might consider making up cue cards on poster board (or, depending on the distance and on how sharp your actors' eyes are, you might be able to repurpose an iPad).

If you'll be doing the same piece several times to try to get the best take, it's important to have a marker at the beginning of each one identifying it for later—that's why you see those black-and-white clapboards with chalk saying things like "Scene 4, Take 2."

But that's only half the puzzle; it's just as important to make sure that somebody in the production is keeping track of how each take went. If an actor flubs a line in every five-minute take but the seventh one, it'll be much faster to skim your notes to find the star and the comment "all lines OK" written by take 7 than it will be to watch all of those scenes over again.

You'll also want someone acting in the role of a script or continuity supervisor to make sure everything stays visually consistent down to the last detail. A scar on an actor's left cheek should not suddenly migrate to the right cheek in shooting on another day. A door that was closed for one take shouldn't be open in the next, or it'll be harder to merge those takes smoothly in editing.

In general, there are four basic technical things you need to pay close attention to with recorded video content in order to look as if you know what you're doing (and two that you need to watch with recorded audio as well).

1. **Focus and lighting.** Focus, of course, is how sharp your image is; bad focus leads to video that is either entirely blurry or blurry in just the spots you need to be clearest. Consumer-grade recorders typically have an autofocus feature that will manage this for you; double-check that it's working the way you need it to before you move ahead very far.

    Lighting and shadow is also crucial. Natural light in an indoor setting can give a warm feeling to recorded video, while fluorescents can make it feel cold and stark—and may even introduce a distracting flicker. In general, you'll want to be careful to make sure the light is facing in the same direction as your camera, and not toward it, or you'll wind up with a bright background and silhouettes of actors. You may want to use dim lighting for effect. If you do, make sure your camera can accommodate those conditions; you won't want to end a hard day's work and discover that all you've captured is a bunch of voice-overs on top of blackness.

2. **Framing.** This refers to what's included in the shot and how it's centered. You'll most often want to make sure that framing is fairly close, both so that you can clearly make out the actors' performances and so that you don't include a lot of extraneous and potentially distracting space. There are artistic reasons for using more distant or offset framing; if you plan to use these methods, understand what you're doing and why.

3. **Background noise.** Crickets chirping, an ambulance in the background, a house being demolished next door—these can all create an unacceptable amount of background noise in your recorded audio or video. This can have results ranging from making it hard to hear your intended content to distracting the audience; at worst, the audience might even think the noise is a clue to something else. If you don't have access to a soundproofed studio, at least try to record at times of day and in locations where you're least likely to be interrupted by background noise.

4. **Editing.** This is what turns your rough recorded footage into something special and polished. Once upon a time, you needed specialty equipment to do film or audio editing; now anyone with an Apple computer and iMovie or GarageBand can make a go of it. Don't skip this step and just put a single take out there without at least considering whether you should trim it, merge scenes together, or mix and match different takes to get a better whole.

STORYTELLING IN THE BACKGROUND

Decisions on casting, setting, and production values all provide context that casts light on your story for the audience.

If you come from a text background, it can come as a surprise to discover the minutiae in film production that must be proactively chosen. Questions that you can leave ambiguous in text must be clear on film—and not just the obvious stuff, like how long a character's hair is and whether he's more likely to wear a T-shirt and trench coat or a hand-knit holiday sweater. The demands of film mean that you need to establish what time of day or night it is; whether the scene is indoors or outdoors; how fast lines are delivered; what kind of weather there is; and even what kind of person occupies the space you shoot in, because that characterization must be reflected in the set.

Casting, too, is clearly an important vector for characterization. How you cast will depend on story, budget, and timing factors, but let me urge you not to cast friends in your key roles, unless they have a solid history of acting in other projects. You're likely to overestimate the quality of a friend's performance and will be unlikely to give heavy direction, even if it proves necessary.

Set dressing is also a vehicle for characterization, when it's done right. Video set in a character's home is going to give you a very different vibe if the backdrop is a blank wall or if the wall is blanketed with posters for metal bands. A china cabinet full of cherubic figurines tucked in the back corner will leave you with a different impression from a bookcase full of gilt-edged and leather-bound tomes. Your camera's-eye view into an office might see a cluttered cube stuffed with papers, a wooden desk overgrown with potted plants, or a completely clear glass surface with only a single photograph on it. And each of these possibilities will have implications for your wider story, because it's establishing something about your world, and you're going to need to know what that is if you are to keep everything internally consistent.

So as with all other elements of transmedia production, you have to pay attention to every detail of what the audience sees, because it becomes a part of your story, for good or ill. You have to make sure that the message your audience receives isn't inadvertently undermining what you actually meant to convey.

Even the quality of the footage you shoot says something about your story. If you aren't an expert at video production and you don't have the cash to hire an expert crew, your best bet is to stick with shooting content where an amateurish cast is not just forgivable, but expected—vlogs shot from someone's home, for example, or action recorded by a character on a consumer camcorder while she flees from danger. Nobody would expect such video to look as good as a lush Hollywood production.

On the other hand, if you're new to video production, you'll want to stay away from filming fictitious news broadcasts and press conferences or action sequences, which will look unconvincing if you don't have a good set and budget behind them.

DISTRIBUTION

Getting your video content distributed as a movie in theaters or aired on television as a show is a complicated business, and if you're interested in pursuing those avenues, you're better off seeking out an authority specific to the channel you're hoping to obtain. (Though if you're willing to pay, you can choose to distribute video or audio content as advertising on TV, on the radio, or even in movie theaters.) But those are by far not the only routes for distributing this kind of content.

Many transmedia projects stick to online-only distribution through video-sharing or podcasting sites. This is the least expensive method, but it also comes with a few issues. YouTube puts limits on how long an uploaded file can be, for example. Note that as of this writing, Vimeo's limit is a lot longer.

If you're developing an application for a mobile device, you can integrate video into that; if you do, though, you'll probably need to lower the quality of your recorded video to reduce the file size. That's because video files can be big. Really big. Higher quality and longer run times will make those video files even bigger. Take this into consideration when making backups and transferring data—you might do better sending a courier across town with an external hard drive than with a shared drive or an FTP server.

23

Bringing Your Story into the Real World

Multiple media are fantastic, but the ultimate platform is the real world. Some of the splashiest transmedia stories use live events that take place in a real location and physical artifacts to convey story information.

Live story events in particular can be mind-blowing for the lucky fraction of your audience that's close enough to attend (or, in the case of a live but online event, in the right time zone). If you plan to have a live event as a part of your transmedia experience, though, it's important that you think very carefully about the parameters of what you're planning: whom you expect to attend, how they'll find out about it and get there, how long you expect them to stay actively involved, and how you'll signal to them when it's all over.

In general, there are two kinds of live events: those that take place at a physical location, and those that take place virtually. In both cases, you need to be keenly aware that no matter when or where you hold your event, you're locking out a lot of potential audience members.

It's common nowadays to split the difference and hold a series of similar live events in multiple geographic locations—*Why So Serious?* and its cake and pizza partnerships, for example, allowed would-be players from across the country to have a chance at playing, on top of its showy presence at places like Comic-Con. It's also increasingly common (and good design) to have an online component to a live physical event, so that committed players can participate without ponying up hundreds of dollars for a plane ticket.

A clue from the *Why So Serious?* Comic-Con event in 2007

Copyright Steve Peters. Used with permission.

Planning a physical live event is a lot like planning a wedding. You need to make sure you have a time and place; you have to make sure to invite your guests far enough in advance that they can arrange to get there; and you have to have your activities planned down to the last detail.

Generally, it's good form to hold a physical event on a weekend, when people are much less likely to have a conflict with work or school. And if you pick early afternoon on the East Coast of the United States—say, at 2 or 3 p.m.— you access a fairly broad swath of time zones. After all, 2 p.m. on the East Coast is 11 a.m. on the West Coast and still only 7 p.m. in the United Kingdom.

If you're trying for something truly international, though, you might try to structure an event that plays out over eight or more hours, or periodically around the clock for several days, to make sure that each wedge of the time zone pie feels a little love from you.

The performative elements of a live event can be difficult to manage. Events that take place using actors are incredibly powerful. This can be at an actual place (a park, a concert, or wherever), over the phone, or even through streaming video.

The key to holding this kind of event successfully is to make sure that you hire actors who are very, very comfortable with improvisational work. Then you have to make sure that they're very, very aware of the ins and outs of their characters, what they can and can't say, and how they should react to specific questions.

Rehearsing a live event ahead of time, and preferably multiple times, is a must to work out any kinks in your plan. It's also helpful to create a detailed timeline of what you expect to unfold over the course of the event, detailing in short intervals what each character on the scene should be doing, and also what actions you expect the audience to take. This will help your pacing, as you'll be able to visually spot if too many things are going on at the same time, or if there are long periods when your audience will be at a loose end, and maybe bored.

I find it helpful to plan a live event with a number of pre-scripted set pieces: an argument between two characters, say, or the response you want primed for a particular question the character is likely to get. I've heard some designers plan (and presumably execute) elaborate plans involving a writer quickly scribbling down lines for the actor on the fly, but this is a method that's very prone to error, or at least to coming off as stilted. It's far better to be comfortable with the actor's ability to own his character for the duration of the event.

It's simpler if you're running an online event that will be mostly text—a chat room, say, or other kinds of instant messaging. In those cases, you can simply have the writer on deck acting as the character.

Be warned, though, that this kind of performative writing is an intense and addictive experience. Once you've done it, you may never want to go back to the slow and low-feedback cycle of writing something alone and finally putting it in front of an audience months or years later.

Then again, some kinds of online events cheat the system a little bit to make them look live when they really aren't live at all. In *Routes*, we used preshot video loops tailored to an online application that looked like a security camera system. The audience had to perform a series of online tasks, and it looked as if they were helping a team of teenagers to break into a biopharmaceutical laboratory. But in reality, all of the video had been shot the week before, and when the players completed each task successfully, a watchful moderator simply triggered the next piece of video in the sequence.

The illusion that everything was completely live was aided by the fact that we'd invited some players to take part in this lab raid, and video of the invited players was interwoven at the beginning and end of the event. (They were keeping watch outside after giving the main characters in the story a distraction to help them get in.) This gave credence to the impression that the entire event was being livestreamed. But in reality, even that was partly smoke and mirrors; the event we played out for the invited players occurred a full hour before the online event, and their video components were edited in at the last minute to work smoothly with our existing preshot video.

PHYSICAL ARTIFACTS

Live events aren't the only way the story can manifest in the physical world. Objects that purport to be from a story world can be deeply meaningful to an audience. These can be newspapers, postcards, paintings, ceramic masks, statuettes . . . there really is no end to the possibilities.

Commissioning a propmaker to create limited runs of these objects can make a very meaningful memento for a few players; manufacturing and retailing them can be the cornerstone of an ongoing business model.

Few things can bring a player the sense of wonder and connection to the story as receiving a tangible piece of it. It's rewarding, and not just in the sense of receiving compensation. In some cases, the physical artifact is a motivation—for example, a treasure hunt for an object, as in *Masquerade*, Levi's *Go Forth*, and *The Clock Without a Face*.

You can also use physical artifacts as a way for your audience to interact with the story. Lance Weiler's *Pandemic* experience incorporated a treasure hunt for water bottles and golden objects; the team also created a number of "bear totems," which incorporated a camera, an MP3 player, a slide viewer, and a thumb drive and were used to both convey story information and capture the player's reactions to it.

Creating such a complex bespoke item is a costly endeavor. However, physical artifacts don't have to be expensive. Printed comics and books aren't (so far) widely used elements of transmedia, but they're still tools in the box that

The bear totem for *Pandemic*
Used with permission of Lance Weiler

you should be aware of. For small or independent projects, resources like Lulu.com can be sufficient. (Although if the option is available to you, working with an established publisher will help you produce a more polished and much more widely distributed product.)

Better yet, you can also work with a direct mail house (or even your own printer, in a pinch) to create inexpensive paper artifacts like newspapers, postcards, and letters at a fairly low production cost. This is arguably one of the least expensive ways to produce a physical artifact. The printed word is a very efficient method for conveying narrative; you can pack a tremendous density of story into an item with very little overall cost.

Other inexpensive artifacts could include small pins or badges, stickers, and the like. These don't cost much to manufacture or to ship, though you'll have to be more inventive for them to carry as much of a story payload.

Be careful when you go down the physical artifact path, however. If you're giving out these items for free, you'll need to decide on a budget and a distribu-

tion method that won't break the bank, but will feel fair to your audience. Nothing can seem as insulting to a player as not receiving a special item when other, less-engaged audience members have.

TELEPHONY

Using the telephone can also be an incredibly powerful and intimate component of a transmedia story. One of the most famous events from *The Beast* was the Mike Royal event, in which players had to call a telephone number for "Statue Security." The Red King, a teenager, had been kidnapped, and the players had traced his location to the Statue of Liberty. Mike Royal was a security guard on shift there, and over the course of a few hours, players had to talk him into risking his job in order to save that boy.

The frisson I got when I called that number and a real human being answered was unforgettable. But there are some caveats to using a live actor, as with any live event. For one thing, you need to make sure that whoever is answering the phone knows his character and his lines inside and out. In *The Beast*'s example, the man on the other end of the line was Sean Stewart, the game's lead writer. Who better to spin the story out as it happened?

And then, of course, there were the busy signals. The line was flooded with people calling in to try their hand at persuading Mike Royal to do the right thing. Live actors just don't scale the way automation does—and people are unaccustomed to hearing a busy signal these days, instead of simply being kicked over to voice mail. An automated system, on the other hand, might be able to handle dozens, hundreds, or maybe even thousands of calls at the same time.

Unfortunately, using the telephone can become a high-cost tool, compared to alternatives like web content. Though not always—if you want to accept inbound calls and simply send them to voice mail, that's low-cost; you can set up a Skype account to handle it and let it be.

USING NEW TECHNOLOGIES

Not being clairvoyant, I will inevitably neglect to address the vast sweep of emerging media and platforms in this book. But there are a few helpful principles you can consider to determine how to work a new technology or media platform into your story (and even whether to do it at all).

1. **Don't rush into a technology before your audience does.** As Six to Start's Adrian Hon says, there's not a lot of point in being a first adopter of a new platform in order to tell your story. A brand-new technology product or service can be unreliable. Twitter's early days were riddled with appearances of the "Fail Whale," for example, which appeared during times when the service was unavailable. And early adoption may leave you with a much smaller pool from which to draw your audience.

   Let's take a concrete example: even now, QR codes are a questionable choice for mainstream work. According to a 2011 Comscore report, only 6 percent of smartphone users in the United States actually scan QR codes, and Nielsen reports that only about a third of mobile phones are smartphones to begin with. Why limit your potential audience to just 2 percent of the population right out of the gate?

   Likewise, any innovative mechanics that require your audience to have expensive or rare equipment should be viewed with deep suspicion. You can definitely make a case for using such bleeding-edge tools (say, to encourage their adoption among your audience). But these are exceptional cases. Using a new technology for the sake of being first to the gate shouldn't be the most-used screwdriver in your toolbox.

   At the end of the day, the only thing you gain from being the first to use a platform for a narrative purpose is a few hours or days of press buzz, and maybe a reputation for being innovative but niche. If adoption isn't widespread enough for that press buzz to translate into a larger audience, you're probably wasting your time and money. *(continued)*

2. **Become an expert.** Before you make a platform a key component of your story, you need to be excruciatingly familiar with its ins and outs.

    For online services, be very clear on what their rules of use are. Read the terms of service carefully to make sure that the purpose you have in mind is allowed—think of how awful it would be to make your whole story, then have key components deleted midway through because of terms of service violations. If it's unclear or if you're pretty sure you're not allowed to use the tool the way you'd hoped, you should still reach out and ask the service's support or PR staff. Sometimes a new business will make an exception or reach a special agreement with you, just for the publicity that being a part of your story can garner it.

    For other kinds of technology, be very sure you know what the requirements are to use it safely and distribute the result to your audience—and be sure to step through the user experience several times, under varying conditions, to make sure it plays out the way you intended. Try to imagine every conceivable way in which something could go wrong, and then test out what happens in those conditions.

3. **Have a plan B.** Did I mention that new technologies can sometimes be unreliable? If you absolutely must use a brand-new product or service in your story, it's a good idea to have a backup plan for propagating those pieces of narrative, just in case your plan doesn't go as expected.

    This is a good idea even when you're using traditional media, of course, but it's even more important if you're doing anything unusual, particularly if you're dealing with a time-sensitive story element. Know what you'll do if the upload takes all night, if the service goes down, if the vendor goes out of business, if the recorder breaks, if the file is corrupted, if the ink runs out, if the electronics get rained on . . . Murphy's Law should be your gospel.

Making outbound calls (usually with a recorded message) is another high-impact tool. To do this, you'll need to find a service that does broadcast calling; there are several of them online, all with different capacities in terms of the number of calls you can make and the size of the commitment they require from you. You'll want to be sensitive to time of day in the time zone you're calling, of course.

There are a few other uses for the phone besides simply making and receiving phone calls. If you have the budget and the technical skills to build a phone tree or incorporate voice recognition, you can include some really immersive mechanics. This can be tricky to set up correctly; make sure you test it thoroughly before you make the phone number public.

Sending out mass text messages, on the other hand, can be a technical and budgeting nightmare. Outbound messages can be quite costly—even 30 cents per message adds up to a lot of money pretty fast. And if you're not quite sure how many participants to expect—well, the budget difference between sending 5,000 messages and 20,000 could sink your entire project. If you absolutely must include a text-messaging component, budget for it very generously.

Q&A: YOMI AYENI

Yomi Ayeni is a transmedia filmmaker whose independent work, like the transmedia film *Breathe*, often challenges the audience with intense content during live events. He is currently in production on *The Clockwork Watch*, a steampunk romance.

Q: *How did you get into transmedia?*

A: I stumbled into what we now call transmedia years ago while developing a reality TV format for a U.K. television company. I'd been asked to find the best way to present a travel adventure so that the audience could live, experience, or relive each adventure through interaction with the participants in far-flung places around the world. The feedback led me to reassess all my media training—it seemed that people were asking for more from their entertainment. They wanted to be part of it, not just buy the T-shirts, get car stickers or badges, or dress up. I went on to win a Broadcast Award for the show, and I realized that there was more to this than appending an email address to a TV show.

Though this project was the tip of the iceberg, it demonstrated the lengths to which people were willing to go—not just to be on TV, but to live within a story universe. My second foray was *Violette's Dream*; the experience cemented my faith in creating participatory concepts that offer the audience access so that it can "tinker" with a "live" story as it unfolds, and use social media to funnel people's individual experiences back into the story.

Q: *You've run some pretty intense live events—how do you keep your players (and actors!) safe and comfortable?*

A: Our motto is and will always be "safety first"; as for comfort, that depends on the nature of the scene, the characters, and the story. Irrespective of the situation, we always have actors in between the participants and harm's way.

We work with theatrical companies that specialize in tactical entertainment; they interact with unsuspecting members of the public every day. We're not talking about pranks, but full daylong experiences in which participants don't realize that they are immersed in a choreographed situation.

During production, we drop volunteers into our rehearsals, watch their reactions, and fine-tune. To be honest, it's a case of trust, and we've been building it up for years.

Our more daring experientials are set up to jolt participants into our universe. They often involve no more than 30 people, who become the sole storytellers of those experiences. Though they are filmed, we never publish the content or even refer to the experience in the course of the project.

We've had waterboarding, held mock assassinations, tested people's trust by asking them to fall backward off platforms six feet off the ground, asked people to step away from their daily lives and go on four-hour adventures far away from their homes—you just wait and see what we have planned for *Clockwork Watch*.

I worked at the BBC for 10 years, and I have been on several health and safety courses, and I have been playing with reality TV formats since 2000. While no one can ever say he has mastered human behavior, I can spot trouble at a distance. My instincts have served me well—and I work with an awesome team of professionals who are worth their weight in gold.

Q: *Do you have any helpful tips for integrating live material with prerecorded content?*

A: One main bit of advice: don't box yourself in by trying to stick to the script. It hardly ever works, and participants are ultra-unpredictable. You can't break people out of the default world, then ask them to follow your preplanned schedule—never! Loosen things up a little and see what happens. The best parts are unscripted. You'll be surprised; just keep the cameras rolling . . .

Q: *How do you account for things going wrong in a live event?*

A: Try not to make things too complex, have a good production/stage manager and a dependable crew, and stick to the plan; that way, if things go wrong, you have enough people to deal with them. So far, I've had only one thing go wrong—no, that's not true; I've had several. Hiccups in *Violette's Dream*—when we couldn't parachute a participant out of a plane over a desert in the United States; a crew member contacting a participant because his phone had run out of battery power; not having enough staff to manage a crowd of more than 1,000 at an event, so we had to find a cameraman at around midnight; a participant stopping a 1 a.m. rooftop assassination.

I learn from my previous mistakes.

SECTION V

THE BIG PICTURE

24

How to Fund Production Costs

*B*eing a starving artist isn't as glamorous as it sounds, and the biggest, boldest transmedia visions require some serious money to realize. So at the end of the day, every transmedia creator needs to think about cold, hard cash.

There are two different levels of financial concern you might have as a transmedia storyteller. Yes, you need money to pay for the resources you'll need for your projects—but you also have to keep yourself housed and fed as you create your masterwork. Before you can begin to make well-informed choices about your future, you'll need to answer an underlying and much deeper question: where does transmedia money come from?

This is one of the most discussed and necessary topics in the creator community, and for good reason: we've hit upon few sustainable business models to date. Let's take a look at the existing revenue models for funding a transmedia project.

When we think about transmedia, most of us think first about commissioned work. This means projects that are funded by a client and executed by an agency, a studio, or a media or production company. Commissioned projects are typically marketing campaigns, but there are some other high-profile examples; No Mimes Media has done a few projects for Cisco that were meant to be innovative team-building exercises, for example. And sometimes a TV channel like Channel 4 in the United Kingdom will commission a production house to shoot a program and integrate transmedia elements. Museums, libraries, and universities have all commissioned location-based transmedia projects, too.

The common thread in these projects is that of a client–producer relationship; one party is paying the other to produce the transmedia experience on its behalf. Generally speaking, the actual transmedia producer isn't the one who will ultimately benefit if the project is a wild success; the client will.

Most commissioned work comes from marketing budgets in one way or another. Either the experience is directly funded with a marketing budget, as for a TV show (which is, in turn, funded by ad dollars), or else the commissioner plans to use the content as a vehicle for advertising (replacing the role of the TV show itself). When MTV commissions an original transmedia experience like *Valemont*, for example, it's because it could get a sponsorship deal with Verizon. Those ad dollars flow to the commissioner, who doles some of them out to the transmedia production company. The cycle of media continues.

There are situations in which the actual creator can profit, too, of course. Big entertainment franchises like *Tron*, *Avatar*, and the like account for even more money than transmedia marketing does. Production costs for these kinds of projects can be covered by investors: private individuals, companies, or film funds, for example. Sometimes production costs will come from a company's existing cash reserves.

A handful of start-ups have obtained production costs from venture capital, too, Fourth Wall Studios being the most notable. Chasing venture capital is a slow and frustrating game, though; if you plan to go that route, make sure that you're not holding your project hostage to the promise of future money. You can start work on the story and even the technology, if necessary, before you get funding. And to be completely honest, no VC worth its salt will give you money if it doesn't look like you've already planted the seeds of your own success.

GOING INDIE

Let's say for the sake of argument that you don't have the business connections or the desire to start an agency and go after commissioned work. And let's hypothesize that you don't have the leverage to get big investments in your transmedia project because you don't have much of a track record, or because your project is naturally small-scale and won't pay off with much profit even in the best case. Not all is lost—there's still a way to get your project made.

1. **Crowdfunding.** This is the process of raising money directly from your would-be audience. Sometimes this takes the form of donations; sometimes it operates a little more like preorders or advance ticket sales. There are a handful of websites out there that you can use to promote your project and collect crowdfunding efforts.

    Kickstarter is one of the most popular, and it is flexible enough to allow a wide variety of projects. The catch with Kickstarter is that you have to set a target amount of money to raise, and if you don't hit your target, you won't get any money at all. There are other sites, too: IndieGoGo, for example, is aimed primarily at helping independent filmmakers to raise money, but more than a few films with a strong transmedia element have made a good showing there.

    Crowdfunding is a great way to build up a small nest egg of capital to pay for pieces of your production that you don't have the skills to produce yourself, as long as you already have an existing base of fans, friends, or family who will be willing to chip in some money to help you out. The amount of money you can raise is seldom very big, though, and you have to be willing to do heavy promotion of your funding efforts.

2. **Grants.** Instead of getting a commercial commission or monetizing your audience, you could apply to any of a number of new media funds and arts grants to fund the transmedia project of your dreams. The Tribeca Film Institute has started a new media fund, for a start, and many traditional grants organizations in the arts community would be interested in funding a transmedia project.

   The application process can be tricky, and competition is generally pretty fierce. Also, the money is likely to come with a lot of strings and caveats. Even if you do win a grant, the money you get probably won't help you pay the rent; you'll be lucky if it covers all the resources you need to build out, with the expectation that all of your labor is free. And grants often come with some very serious reporting requirements—you need to be able to account for every penny you spend, and often for the outcome of the project as well.

   But grant money can help you to build a bigger and better project than if you had no budget at all; it's up to you to decide if it'll be worth it.

3. **Low- and no-budget.** Finally, it's entirely possible to produce your transmedia project with no budget at all, using whatever resources you already have or can borrow. You will generally have to lay out at least a few hundred dollars of your own money for things like domain name registration and hosting, and your production isn't likely to have the same kind of polish as a well-funded one.

   But it absolutely is possible to get an enthusiastic fan community around a project produced mainly with duct tape and borrowed cameras. If your story and structure are high quality, that's all you really need. And if your no-budget project is a success, you can leverage that to move on to

PITCHING

When you're pitching a transmedia project to a potential client, commissioner, or investors, you're going to have to take off your artist hat for a while and instead put on your business goggles.

The one big question you need to answer in your pitch is this: "What's in it for me?"

And (helpful hint here) in general, clients and investors aren't going to be interested in something just because you have an innovative concept for telling a story across multiple media. You're going to have to make a solid case for something a little more robust.

Revenue is the one big thing that a client or investor will always sit up and pay attention to, and the more the better. As Justin Timberlake said in his turn as Sean Parker in *The Social Network*, "A million dollars isn't cool. You know what's cool? A billion dollars."

But money isn't the only promise a pitch should make. Determining what will sway your potential client is key to your success; you need to know what the client is looking for. If you're pitching to a TV channel or movie studio, for example, the people you're talking to will be looking for a strong story concept, and evidence that it can find an audience. You'll need to make sure that you're communicating your storytelling chops effectively.

Sometimes the key to success will be forecasts of engagement, views and impressions, or less concrete metrics like reputation or brand perception; those are what advertisers are looking for. You can't predict the future, of course, but you need to be able to describe how the structure of your project will be fine-tuned to best meet the client's goals.

And no matter whom you're pitching to, you need to inspire confidence that you can execute on the vision you're promising. That means paying close attention to the details of your slides or specification documents, punctuality in deadlines and meetings, and responding to calls and emails promptly. If you can't produce a high-quality pitch document, nobody will believe you can do better at anything bigger.

bigger, better things going forward—like commissioned work, or even getting serious investment to lay the cornerstone of your very own transmedia franchise.

Or maybe, if you find a way to monetize your project once it's built, you can stay indie forever.

Q&A: SARA THACHER

Sara Thacher is an artist and producer who is best known for her work on *Jejune Institute*, an immersive locative art project in San Francisco. She is one of relatively few prominent creators in the transmedia community to come from a fine arts background, rather than film, marketing, or games.

Q: *How did you get into transmedia?*

A: I went to art school. As I studied art history, specifically contemporary sculpture, I started to notice that more and more, the most interesting work came from artists (like Alan Kaprow) who were focused on creating something where the artwork could not exist without the audience. The work actually relied on the audience's active participation in order to happen at all. At the same time, I saw work by artists that used whichever tool was most appropriate to convey the idea and crossed between video, installation, theater, and object making.

Of course, in art school you're expected to actually make things, not just read about them in art history, so I did just that. As I worked on gradually more ambitious projects, I also started looking outside of the "art world" for audiences/participants.

Immediately after grad school, I started working with Jeff Hull on the *Jejune Institute*. This felt like a very natural step from my previous projects. And indeed, while at Nonchalance, we continued to ride the line between creating work that fell within and outside of the art world. We spent our time working on independent projects, arts commissions, and corporate client work, all of which had a focus on creating spaces for the audience to become active participants.

Q: *Are there any little-known methods for getting arts funding?*

A: Most of what I know about this topic is specific to arts funding in the United States, which is increasingly privately driven. However, even as national funding for the arts dwindles, there are local government initiatives that drive the commissioning of new work. These are primarily in the category of "public art"—a term that has fortunately grown to encompass much more than bronze sculptures on plinths in the middle of public parks. Depending on the commissioning group, they may be interested in projects that can, for instance, occupy the screen savers on the computers at the library or change the way people understand the history of a park.

Most art grants that you'll see are project specific, meaning that you apply to the group with a proposal for a specific project that you would like to do. There are a small but growing number of grants that are interested in funding pure research (this can sometimes include travel) or professional development (like purchasing equipment, or hiring a graphic designer to give your business cards and website an updated look). Money often isn't the only factor—if dedicated time or space to work on your project would help, there are a variety of artists' residences that might be a good fit. These can be especially helpful in the early stages of a project, to gain some focused time working out a particular issue among a group of supportive creative people.

Q: *How can a creator make a better case in applying for a grant for a transmedia project?*

A: At one point, I dreaded having to apply for a grant for a project because it didn't fit neatly into the categories given. Providing work samples was an exercise in creativity in and of itself because many of the application forms had no method for reviewing a website—only 35-mm slides. Thankfully, much of that has changed, and digital portfolios are standard. However, it's good to keep in mind that unlike when making a pitch, where you often get to speak directly to the client or at the very least are in control of the format of your deck, when applying for a grant, you are at the mercy of the format of that particular grant application. It's important to follow the requested length for each section and the instructions to the letter, because your project proposal will be reviewed at the same time as hundreds or thousands of others.

To make a truly stunning grant application, you still need to use a little extra creativity to get across the interconnectedness of the media and platforms in your project. Most applications will ask for an "image list" or a "slide sheet"— this is your friend. Typically this is used to share details such as dimensions and medium (for a painting or sculpture) or runtime (for a video). I generally write a short paragraph describing each piece of media (video clip, website, still image, and so on) and how it fits into the larger whole of the project (for example, "This image is a screen capture of a live chat between the players and two of the main characters in the narrative. It allowed players to interact with Character X, who would later appear in a series of video shorts."). Respect the format of the grant application, but look for any opportunity to make that format work for you.

The bigger lesson is that not fitting into neat checkboxes of "sculpture," "video art," "feature film," or even "architecture" is your biggest advantage. Whatever the subject of the grant, 90 percent of the proposals that the organization will be reviewing will most likely have a lot in common with one another because the people who wrote them identify as "sculptors" or "filmmakers." As a transmedia creator, your proposal will stand out. Please don't hear this as an endorsement to run out to NYFA Source (http://www.nyfa.org/source) and apply for every grant and commission opportunity listed; writing a great grant application is a lot of work, and you should select where you apply with care. That said, think creatively about the guidelines for the grant. Check out work that the organization has funded in the past. If it seems like a grant that might embrace your project—go for it.

25

. . . And Maybe Make Some Profit, Too

*I*n general, you don't strictly need to turn a dime in profit directly from commissioned work, but if you have investors—and that might include yourself and the sweat of your brow—then you really need your project to have a revenue stream.

To date, there have been only a few businesses focused on creating stand-alone transmedia entertainment as their core business, and none of them has been a runaway success. Indeed, a successful and ongoing transmedia business model is the industry's holy grail. But just as we borrow production techniques from other disciplines, so should we look to them for other ways to monetize our creations.

The first and most obvious method for monetizing your project is to have your audience pay you directly for content. It works for books and movies, why not for multiplatform narratives? But the subscription model has a checkered history.

The first commercial transmedia story to charge a subscription fee was *Majestic*, an EA video game with the tagline, "It plays you." This highly innovative game played out in episodes over real time, incorporating content via instant messaging, phone calls, faxes, and websites. Its story began with a message to new players that *Majestic* had been canceled—and then players had to unravel the conspiracy behind the cancellation. The game was canceled for real after less than a year because of low player numbers, despite its critical acclaim.

For a long time, the story of *Majestic* soured producers on the idea that audiences would pay for transmedia stories at all. But while that idea still lingers in the industry's subconscious, huge strides have been made in having audiences pay for content in an amazing variety of ways.

DIRECT SALES OF CONTENT

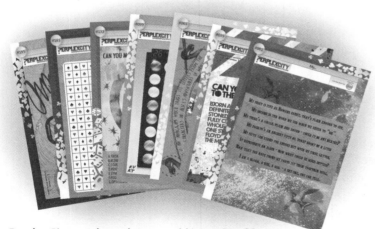

***Perplex City* puzzle cards were sold in packs of five**
Used with permission of Mind Candy

Other early attempts to monetize transmedia projects used the sale of physical artifacts. EDOC Laundry simultaneously told and funded a story with the sale of wearable items like T-shirts and hats. There was also *Perplex City*.

Perplex City was the first commercial alternate reality game (and my first professional gig, too). Packs of puzzle cards sold in stores and online contained references intended to drive players to visit a persistent but fictional online world. *Perplex City* had its own weekly online newspaper, government, and other institutions that existed on the web as if they were real—along with characters who would answer your emails, all in the days before social media. The purpose of the game was a real-world treasure hunt; players had to locate a priceless

artifact that the Perplexians had lost. The clever winner who found it buried in the woods in Southeast England won a reward of $200,000.

The sale of physical items that shed light on the story has also gained traction in the publishing industry. *Cathy's Book,* by Sean Stewart and Jordan Weisman, is one of the most successful transmedia novel experiments to date. The physical book sold in stores included an "evidence folder" of photographs, postcards, and the like. The content included multiple references to expanded content that readers could engage with, including phone numbers players could call to listen to voice mail messages and websites to visit. Jordan Weisman used a similar model in working with J. C. Hutchins on *Personal Effects: Dark Art.*

Light transmedia experiences confined to a single mobile application have made their appearance on the market, too; *Hidden Park* and *Urban Sleuth*, for example. And while a revenue stream for it is not yet clear, Fourth Wall Studios' *RIDES* platform looks poised to offer short paid experiences to audiences that start in a browser window but extend to using the phone, email, and other media.

Live performances that extend into digital spaces can always charge for tickets, of course. *Accomplice*, for example, is an interactive show performed in New York and Los Angeles that takes the audience through a sequence of locations and situations over the course of the show, essentially allowing them to live out a story in small groups. And World Wrestling Entertainment, probably one of the most successful and least-talked-about transmedia enterprises in existence, charges for admission to its matches—with additional revenue streams from TV rights, special pay-per-view bouts, and plenty of merchandising.

The biggest problems with executing pay-to-play are traditional business problems as much as creative ones. Making a compelling story is just the beginning. After that, how do you get a product on shelves or sell tickets? How do you promote? How do you distribute? If you plan to go this way, you'd better have a rock-solid business plan for dealing with these issues—or a partnership agreement with somebody who can do it for you.

MERCHANDISING

Speaking of the WWE and merchandise, merchandising is a revenue stream that gets overlooked a lot, despite its high value for franchises. The value of merchandise for a small, bootstrapped creator can be exceptional.

Consider the example of Andrew Hussie's project, *MS Paint Adventures*. This project is nominally a webcomic, but it doesn't take long to realize that it's a lot more than that. The work in progress, *Homestuck*, is as much text as graphic, and includes music that was custom-composed for the characters and the story. The project also includes occasional Flash animations, and even short interactive elements where the audience can explore an environment in the story with the avatar of one of the characters (or several). And *MS Paint Adventures* is quite interactive—much of the story is presented as though it were a game, with the audience making suggestions about where the story should go next.

MS Paint Adventures does a brisk business in merchandise, from T-shirts and hoodies to pins, art prints, and even plush dolls. And the music, contributed by a team of enthusiastic volunteers, is another revenue stream—several entire albums of music from the project are available.

There is a fairly low barrier to entry for offering merchandise with the advent of online services like Zazzle and CafePress. It's low-cost to simply make a few designs for shirts, posters, and coffee mugs and put them up in a virtual storefront to see how it goes.

ADVERTISING

Advertising money should be a consideration for noncommissioned indie work, too. There are two kinds of advertising to look at: overt ads and product placement. *MS Paint Adventures* incorporates quite a few banner ads into the site, for example.

Overt ads are a mixed blessing. They're easy to implement; you don't have to prove you'll have an audience in advance to put Google ads on your websites. But they can look distracting and unprofessional, and they aren't going to make you very much money unless you're getting an awful lot of traffic. In the cost/benefit analysis, I come down against banner ads and the like; your mileage may vary.

Hussie can get away with it because the overall site isn't fictional in nature; but running ads on your protagonist's personal weblog can be jarring and can cheapen the overall look and feel. It's better to keep ads away from entirely fictional spaces, unless you can present a reasonable in-story reason for them to be there. (And even then, you should give serious thought to running fictional ads instead, or in addition, the better to build out your world.)

Product placement can, in theory, be a little more elegant. You won't be able to get a product placement deal unless you can prove you have a pretty good audience going already, though. The only transmedia project or ARG I'm aware of that has done product placement was *lonelygirl15*, and the execution was awfully heavy-handed, presumably because *lonelygirl* didn't have a lot of bargaining power. I don't think this revenue stream has yet been explored the way it could be.

Finally, there is the sponsorship angle. There haven't been many sponsorship deals thus far in transmedia, but the main caveat is the same as for product placement: your chances of getting a deal hinge entirely on proving that your content is worth the sponsor's time and money. Both sides have to receive value from the transaction.

DONATIONS

One of my favorite transmedia-lite projects, *Shadow Unit*, puts out its content for free, with only a tip jar. *Shadow Unit* is the work of a handful of award-winning science fiction authors who have fans of their work built in, teaming up to write, as they call it, "fan fiction for a show that never existed."

I don't know how much money they've made from the project, but it's certainly not millions. It's not even enough for them to live off of; the creators are all still primarily working hard on other projects. And even so, it's certainly more than you're

likely to make if you go down this road, since you're unlikely to have the fan base of an award-winning science fiction author in your pocket.

Still, there are advantages to this approach. By creating zero barriers to entry for their content, the writers for *Shadow Unit* (and like-minded single-platform artists like Amanda Palmer, Jonathan Coulton, and Cory Doctorow) are making it easier to get new, enthusiastic audience members. As the audience size grows, the odds of being able to monetize the project in other ways down the pike grow more significant— by getting a book or movie deal based on their content, for example. If you give it a try, you won't be rolling in bucks, but you might be able to bankroll the resources you use to create more work, and in turn climb the ladder to making money through sponsorships, subscriptions, and merchandise.

Ultimately, all of this hinges on your ability to attract and hold an audience that values your content enough to plunk down some money. All the revenue streams in the world won't help you if you aren't making something that somebody wants to be a part of.

Q&A: EVAN JONES

Evan Jones worked on the International Emmy-winning project *ReGenesis*, a TV series with groundbreaking interactive components. He went on to cofound Stitch Media, the studio behind award-winning projects like *Remix Redress*, *Moderation Town*, and *The Drunk and On Drugs Happy Funtime Hour*.

Q: *Where do you see the art and business of storytelling headed over the next few years?*

A: More than anything, I see it gaining legitimacy. I've joked for years about the "hierarchy of media" where theater directors are high art and game designers are low art. It's amazing to watch the video-games industry eclipse Hollywood in revenue, yet very few people can name any of the creative minds the way

Entertainment Tonight profiles film festivals. I very much believe that the people furthest ahead of the curve are the audiences, who continually surprise me with how far they're willing to engage the right story at the right time. As business models emerge, I also see a collision on the horizon, where art and entertainment and branding and marketing are all getting muddled together—it seems some days that it's a new frontier and every sector wants to reinvent itself as "storytellers." Stories are very elastic and universal things, though, and I think they'll accommodate all of these in some form.

What I notice about a lot of "future projections" is that they are anticipating that someone will crack the elusive nut of a business model. I'm not waiting around for that day, and I think it's odd to see transmedia incorporate every aspect of media history without thinking that it might also include every conceivable business model, too. Over the next few years, we might come to terms with that. If you want to make something and you can charge money for it, go for it. If someone else is going to become a patron of your work, perfect. The earliest web set up a mindset that it was a phone book or a library card or a direct mailing—all things that we assumed were "free." The value of stories isn't decreasing, but the scarcity of them is, and it's thrown us for a temporary loop.

Q: *What would you recommend that transmedia creators learn about to improve their craft?*

A: What are you better at than anyone else, and what should you never attempt again? Overwhelmingly, transmedia has shown me that it's a team effort. I started my career as an "all-in-one" web monkey, and it is tantalizing to think that there could be an "auteur culture" in transmedia. The best stuff I work on and see from others has strong teams that know where they want to collaborate.

The other homework I'd assign is to make sure that you love transmedia. I've never met an author who doesn't love books or a director who doesn't love film. Because this is a relatively undefined and evanescent space, it's hard to seek out the "classics," but I would raise alarms for creators who don't find themselves immersed in other people's transmedia projects. I'm constantly fascinated by other people's work in this field and flipping back and forth between producer and consumer all the time.

Q: *What made you decide to start your own business?*

A: A thousand different reasons, but the only one that's relevant to this conversation is that I found I was bursting with new ideas and needed to start focusing my attention on those. I had learned through amazing mentors how to do nearly every aspect of a project, and I saw a clear path ahead with Stitch Media.

Q: *What should you consider before you open shop?*

A: So many answers to this question . . . Over the past five years, I have certainly earned an MBA with the intense learning on the fly. Anyone with any business theory or experience at all would laugh at my mistakes—so much so that I find a good portion of my time is now spent on the business matters of my company rather than the creative freedom that generated the company. It's a very important point for all creators who want a company to form around their ideas— being an entrepreneur is not a part-time job. It would also have been nice to have had some sort of capital before I started (but I realize now that I wouldn't have spent it wisely). Building up a dedicated team with equipment to do the job was a significant investment, and those are hard costs that somebody has to pay while you wait for the final payment on your first project.

Q: *How competitive is it out there for a start-up?*

A: It's competitive, and that's a good thing. Nobody should ever start a business that no one else wants. At the same time, though, it's confusing—the media landscape is converging, and it's revealing a lot of overlap. When I want a great transmedia story, do I engage an agency or a broadcaster or a studio or a production company or an artist? Even I don't know the answer to this, and you'll see that the hardest job many start-ups have in this field is educating the market about what they really *do*.

26

Forging Your Own Transmedia Career

***O**n the personal level, there are three ways to make a living if you want to be a transmedia* professional: you can be a freelancer, working for whatever media company, nonprofit, ad agency, or other client has a project that month, maybe even moonlighting from a day job; you can find an in-house job as an employee at the sort of company that does transmedia work; or you can go the entrepreneurial route and start up your own studio or agency. Let's focus on what options are on the table if you want a career in transmedia storytelling.

The first step in building a career is breaking in. One of the most common routes into transmedia so far has been to invent it—and I'm not being flip. Many, many creators have stumbled into using the methods that we now call *transmedia* while chasing after ways to make their projects more innovative, immersive, net-native, engaging, sticky, interactive, or viral. These creators have found themselves

forging separate trails into unknown territory, only to find that others are there before them. If you're reading this book, that horse has bolted from the stable. We know about transmedia, and we want to make a living that way. But how?

Should you try some combination of looking for freelance work and doing your own original material? If you do your own original work, how do you monetize it? Or, is your own work really just a tryout for a payday down the line?

Unfortunately, there is no one true answer. "How to make a career" is just an umbrella question covering a flowchart of possibilities, and how you build your transmedia career is going to depend quite a lot on what you're good at and the risks you're comfortable taking.

FREELANCING IN TRANSMEDIA

Freelancing on a per-project basis is a relatively easy way to sidestep to a transmedia career, because a company doesn't feel like it has to take a big risk and make a permanent commitment to try you out. And not every company does enough transmedia-focused projects to justify hiring a full-time (or even part-time) employee, anyway.

On the personal side of the equation, a little light freelancing is something that you can generally do without quitting your day job or school. It's also extremely helpful to see how different companies operate from the inside; you can learn a variety of best practices and philosophic approaches that can improve your work more rapidly than if you stayed in a single workplace.

To get freelancing work in the first place, though, you need to have a skill to sell, whether it be writing, production, technical development, or web design. You also need to have a portfolio that demonstrates your skill. If you have no applicable background, then your first step has to be making something—a series of websites, some light video, a puzzle trail, an interactive toy; the concept doesn't matter so much as the tangible proof that you can come up with a concept and see it through to execution.

Once you have something you're proud of in your portfolio, you need to start meeting potential clients. It's easy to veer into salesmanship when you meet someone with hiring power. But a client can sense when you look at him and see dollar signs; it's extremely off-putting. Don't think of anyone as a potential source of cash. Think of potential clients as allies and collaborators, or even friends. And don't write off anyone just because he doesn't have the power to sign a contract—you might be surprised at who might have the power to recommend you for a job. It's a great idea to cultivate a network of others who are doing the same work as you. They can refer work to you that they can't do for some reason, and you should, of course, return the favor.

To get to the point of meeting people who can hire or recommend you, you're probably going to have to begin participating in the transmedia community. But there's a catch-22: the things that make you higher-profile and introduce you to a wider community—engaging in creator's communities online, attending meetups and conferences, blogging and podcasting—don't actually make you better at the work, nor do they generally result in dollars lining your pockets.

And never forget that if you have no work to show proving you can walk the way you talk, nobody will hire you, no matter how much of a self-proclaimed expert you are.

Freelancing Is Hard 〜

Let me be very straight with you: it's rough out there. Richard Morgan's *The Awl* essay "Seven Years as a Freelancer, or, How to Make Vitamin Soup" was heartbreakingly resonant with me, because of its accurate portrayal of life as a freelancer. I recommend that you Google it and read the whole thing.

A freelancer is never entirely sure where the next project is coming from. Even when you're working, you're never entirely sure when the next check is going to hit your mailbox. I've been paid up front and on time, and I've been paid (sadly, more often) long months after the project was over and forgotten. It plays havoc with your budget.

You don't get benefits like health insurance or a retirement plan, unless you pay for them out of your own pocket. In lean times, you don't qualify for unemployment benefits. When it's rough, it's really, really rough—and you can never be sure how much time you have until things look bad for you again.

Let me be starkly clear. I think it's fair to call myself a successful transmedia writer and designer. I have a few notable successes under my belt and lots of sparkly awards on my résumé. I have amicable contacts in TV networks, movie studios, media companies, and digital agencies. And even so, I still find myself staring at stretches of time with no work lined up with alarming regularity. Sure, someone might come along and book me through this month, or next month, or even through next year. But then again, they might not.

If you're considering dipping into transmedia freelancing, take a hard look at what I've said here and decide whether it's something you can deal with. Some people aren't cut out for that kind of uncertainty, and there is no shame in that.

How Much Should I Charge? ⌒

It can be terrifying to work out the rates you should be charging as a freelancer. The International Game Developer's Association's special interest group on alternate reality games ran a survey in 2009 trying to establish some ballpark figures, but instead discovered that rates are all across the board, and around half of the work wasn't paid for at all.

Some of this is because the responsibilities that you're likely to have will vary markedly from company to company, and even from project to project, so a blanket one-size-fits-all approach will fit everyone badly. And what a copywriter can charge, an art director can charge, and a technology lead can charge will all be markedly different.

If the role you'll be filling would be functionally the same even if a project were single-medium, then you should investigate the going rates for that role and charge something in line with those rates, your own experience, and your location. Web designers should charge the going rate for web design, LAMP developers should charge their going rate, and so on.

If you're filling a specialty transmedia role, though, then establishing your rates gets a little trickier. You need to take into account who the client is, how hard the client will be to work with, how senior you'll be on the food chain, and how long the project will last.

You can generally charge a little more money for short-term projects and less for longer-term projects. Think of it as giving the client a volume discount in exchange for the stability of knowing where your money is coming from for a while.

You should also take into account what you know of the client. A movie studio, TV network, or national consumer brand will expect to pay more in order to get the most talented professionals—and if you're not charging enough, they may assume you're not at the top of the field. Go for the brass ring; if it's too high, they'll make a counteroffer.

A nonprofit group, a small game studio, or an independent film, though, simply won't have the money to pay the same rates. You should take that into consideration, too, especially if it's a project you'd be really passionate about working on, a cause you really believe in, or a project that promises enough prestige and attention to pop your career up to the next level. (But don't consider it to the extent that you have trouble keeping the lights on—no amount of exposure pays the bills.)

You should also consider how your interactions with the potential client have gone so far. If you find a client incredibly frustrating to communicate with in your first meetings, this is likely to continue through an entire project. It's a good idea to pad your quote a little in such cases to make up for the stress and the extra time you're likely to spend in dealing with that ongoing frustration.

And of course if you're freelance, you'll be on the hook to cover self-employment taxes as required by your national and local governments. In the United States, it's a good idea to take between a quarter and a third of your income and set it aside to pay your quarterly estimated taxes. Getting on the wrong side of the IRS is never fun.

All that said, I know some of you would like to get some solid numbers, just to have something to begin with. So here it is: never accept less than $350 a day—and especially not if you're in a contributing creative role in a commercial or for-profit transmedia project based in a major media hub like New York or Los Angeles. (I'll make an exception if you have absolutely nothing in your portfolio yet.)

Even that number is for a creator who may just be contributing low-level writing or interaction design, but isn't the lead creator. Once you have some experience and your role in a project becomes more senior and more central, your rate can ratchet up past $700 per day, and even more than that. Truly in-demand creators can command consulting fees well into four figures.

PERMANENT EMPLOYMENT

As the field grows and thrives, a growing number of companies are preferring to bring their talent in-house or work exclusively with existing employees. It might make more sense in your situation to go for a job doing transmedia work inside a company that offers regular paychecks and health insurance.

On the other hand, a lot of my colleagues who sometimes do transmedia work at their regular jobs do precious little of it. There is a small, though growing, number of companies out there that focus on transmedia, alternate reality games, pervasive and social games, and so on. But in the grand scheme of things, there aren't that many, and they're mostly small and not hiring right now. It's comparatively easier to get a job with a digital agency, a media production company, a film studio, or a TV network, where you may sometimes get to do some transmedia work (though not as often as you'd like).

If your heart and soul are set on doing all transmedia all the time, the bulk of the available permanent jobs out there are going to frustrate the living daylights out of you. But consider the tremendous advantages: getting paid on a predictable schedule, much simpler taxes, health insurance, paid vacation days, and, if the worst happens . . . unemployment checks. Oh, luxury!

If this sounds like a path you're more comfortable pursuing, your best bet is to hone your employability in a closely related industry—social media marketing, say, or film production. Then demonstrate your interest and skill in transmedia in front of the people who can give a project the go-ahead after you've been hired. Setting yourself up to make a lateral move is going to be easier and safer than trying to get hired as, say, an ad agency's transmedia creative director right off the bat.

But maybe you're already employed by a company that could be making transmedia stories, but isn't. In that case, it's time for you to innovate and pitch internally as much as you can. For every project you touch, imagine a way to apply the transmedia toolset to make the project more immersive, more interactive, more expansive, and more compelling. Make up PowerPoints and storyboards like they're going out of style. Tell your ideas to your boss or your team. Then do it again on the next project. And then the next one.

At worst, you'll be shot down because of concerns over budget, resource allocation, or profit margin, or because it just doesn't fit what the company's trying to do. (Well, OK, you might also become That Annoying Transmedia Guy Who Won't Shut Up.) You might have to develop a thick skin, and you might have a long slog ahead of you before anything sticks. But remember, you'll still get better at using your tools just by planning, even if you never build out a project. (Some companies may let you build out some of your ideas on a small scale for portfolio pieces, too; use your judgment.)

And if you do persuade your company to take a gamble and try one of your ideas, you just might win big. It's like the lottery: you can't ever win if you don't ever play.

Q&A: J. C. HUTCHINS

J. C. Hutchins is a transmedia writer who first rose to prominence by incorporating multimedia and collaborative elements into his smash hit podcast novel, *Seventh Son*. His ability to hustle for and garner press attention and freelance work is legendary, and well worth learning from.

Q: *How did you get into transmedia?*

A: Back in 2006, I was using emerging technologies to release a few of my unpublished novels online for free, in an effort to build an audience for my fiction. The strategy worked—in addition to engaging with tens of thousands of fans, I got on the radar of an editor at St. Martin's Press. He liked my work, and how I was releasing it.

A year later, he reached out to me when an unusual "transmedia novel" project came into his hands: *Personal Effects: Dark Art*, conceived by legendary game designer and transmedia storytelling pioneer Jordan Weisman. As a casual fan of alternate reality games and role-playing games, I was a huge fan of his stuff. St. Martin's was looking for a coauthor on the book, and asked me to put my name into the hat.

A few weeks later, I was working with Jordan on the book. We had an aggressive deadline to plot and write the novel, and to design and execute *Personal Effects'* ambitious "beyond the book" narrative. It was my trial by fire, as I was learning transmedia storytelling best practices along the way.

That book was published in 2009. In 2010, I became a freelance transmedia storyteller, helping marketing agencies and entertainment companies expand and enhance their fictional story worlds.

Q: *Can you tell me a little about your favorite projects?*

A: The *Personal Effects* transmedia project will always be close to my heart, as will *Join the Colony*, a project for which I am credited as cocreator and lead writer. I worked with the agency Campfire to create a transmedia prequel narrative for a Discovery Channel show called *The Colony*. The conceit of that series: 90 percent of the world's population is killed by a viral outbreak, and the remaining 10 percent must work together to survive.

Our job was to create a convincing prequel story that used real science and social media networks in interesting ways, to show how a pandemic might spread . . . and how people might share that news with their friends and loved ones. The project gave me the opportunity to combine my passion for fiction, journalism, filmmaking, and online communication with my deep familiarity with social media networks.

At the time of this writing, another Campfire project I've been working on for months—which expands the story world and promotes the TV miniseries *Bag of Bones*, based on the acclaimed Stephen King novel—will soon debut online. Between the incredible experience of researching and creating content in my favorite author's world and the beyond-cool afternoon working one-on-one with actor Pierce Brosnan for the project, it's been an incredibly memorable experience.

Q: *What would you recommend that transmedia creators learn about to improve their craft?*

A: The best transmedia storytellers are Swiss Army Knives — they're blessed with a knack for adaptability and the ability to tell stories in several media.

Aspiring transmedia creators must identify storytelling forms that they're not familiar with, and dig into them. Be more than a novelist or a short story writer. Become a screenwriter, a journalist, a photographer, a videographer. While you need not be a maestro in each medium, you should have a working vocabulary—or, even better, fluency—in them.

Study the strengths and weaknesses of each medium, and think hard about how to craft narratives that leverage the very best each medium has to offer. Complex expositions are best left to text—but text can never capture a moment as exquisitely as a photograph. Photographs can't deliver the arresting immediacy of video or audio. And none of these media can rival experiencing the story firsthand, in the field. You must bake these compelling opportunities into the DNA of the transmedia stories you're telling if you want them to succeed.

Finally, follow the transmedia storytelling space and the creators making entertainment there. You'll learn best practices . . . and "what not to wear," as well.

Q: *In a crowded media landscape, how do you get your work noticed?*

A: Crow about it. Tell your fans and online followers about it. Get them to tell their friends about it. Many creatives are shy, or fear they'll sound like blustery carnival barkers if they self-promote. I hail from a different mindset: what good is a story if no one's around to experience it? If my goal is to have as many people as possible experience a narrative I helped create, I'm ethically obligated to share it with as many people as I can.

   If you want your work noticed by folks who can get you paid work in the transmedia storytelling space—such as creative directors at agencies, editors at publishing houses, or entertainment executives—your approach should be the same: tell them about your stuff. Reach out with complimentary emails, tip them off to your creative work, and if you're particularly aggressive with your salesmanship, reconnect with them every quarter to remind them of your availability.

Q: *What's the key to managing a successful freelance career?*

A: Busting your ass. Know your worth, charge a fair wage, work hard, and overdeliver on your keepers' expectations. When you dazzle your clients, you become memorable. Memorable freelancers get repeat business. Repeat business keeps your belly full and the lights on.

27

Critical Legal and Ethical Considerations

At first glance, ethics might seem like a funny sort of topic for a book about storytelling. But transmedia ethics are a very serious business, both from the standpoint of doing the right thing by your audience, and from the not-as-squishy perspective of running a business and avoiding liability and litigation. (If you can find a way to cover the cost, insuring your project or yourself with errors and omissions coverage is a good idea.)

There are, of course, a few traditional areas of legal concern that are familiar to anyone who has worked in media before (copyright, for example, and libel) but when you play out a fictional narrative using the real world as your platform, sometimes this has new and unintended consequences.

As a transmedia creator, you have a heavy burden of responsibility toward both your audience and those who stumble onto your work out

of context. That's because some people are inevitably going to think that pieces of it are real. Projects walking the wrong side of that line have been sued for tens of millions of dollars, attracted undesired police attention, or even been denounced by NASA (this has happened to more than one transmedia project!).

Take, for example, the story of the Toyota Matrix *Your Other You* campaign. It was intended as a way for someone to play a prank on a friend. You'd sign up your friend, and she'd receive a few days of personalized messages indicating that one of a variety of menacing characters was on his way to her house—a one-person transmedia experience.

What would you do if you really thought a serial killer was coming to your house? In this case, one of the victims of the prank was genuinely terrified—and when it was revealed as just a practical joke, she sued Toyota and its ad agency, Saatchi & Saatchi, for $10 million.

But let's say you're not trying to play a trick on anyone. Let's say you just want to tell truly deep, immersive stories, stories that are so embedded in the fabric of the real world that it's impossible to tell where fiction begins and reality leaves off. Stories where you can't find the beginning once you start digging for the history, where websites and social media presences go back for months, or even years.

That's what Steve Diddle was trying to do with his Martin Aggett character, whom he created as an interactive social media presence that was indistinguishable from a real person.

It's easy to see the appeal. If a little bit of realism makes the connection to characters feel strong and more relevant, surely even more realism will make it even better, right? Or, as Steve Diddle put it, "I thought that when the game launched and people discovered that someone with whom they'd interacted for months was a fictional character, they would be excited to participate in the game. In hindsight, I realize that was a very naive hypothesis."

Martin Aggett made a lot of friends who thought he was a real person and genuinely liked him. Ultimately, these friends encouraged him to attend an annual convention of ARG players. "It was then that I realized that if I attended ARGfest in character as Martin and made real friendships and connections with people, they would feel betrayed and foolish when I revealed Martin to be fictional," Diddle said.

So Diddle came clean: Martin wasn't a real person. The fallout was ugly. The people Martin had befriended didn't think they had been part of a delightful, long-term immersive experience; they felt betrayed, because someone they thought was a friend had been lying to them about . . . everything.

If there is anyone in the world who would accept that kind of long, deep immersion with delighted surprise, it would be those in the ARG community, who crave pervasive and immersive fiction. If even that audience found it unappetizing, there is absolutely no hope for a mainstream audience. Make sure your players know where the edges of your fiction lie; it's akin to getting informed consent.

Even with informed consent, there are a number of non-negotiable areas in which the audience should be able to trust you. These include not asking your players to do anything illegal or physically dangerous as a part of your game, or allowing ambiguity that might lead them astray into risky territory. If you don't do a good job of that, players will do things that you would never expect them to—and that you would never in a million years want them to do, either.

THE BYSTANDER PROBLEM

There is also some risk of harm to innocent bystanders who might come across pieces of a transmedia experience out of context and think they are for real. For example, a staged kidnapping might seem ethically sound if all the members of your audience know what's going on—but what about the person who sees it from a window and calls the police?

Or imagine that you're telling a story in which a pharmaceutical company carries a major plot point. As one does in transmedia storytelling, you decide to build out the world by creating a website for this company.

For extra verisimilitude, you try to give your fictional pharmaceutical company the same kind of gloss you find on a real company's site, complete with stock photos

of happy people running through meadows and a section of press releases detailing the company's recent advances.

This means you need to fabricate a few medical advances that sound plausible but are not so eye-catching that they draw away from the main thrust of your plot, whatever that might be. Hmm, maybe something about stem cells, something about Parkinson's disease . . . great. So you write up a hundred words saying that Fictional Pharma Company has just finished clinical trials on an innovative treatment for Parkinson's, and the results were very positive, showing a whopping 38 percent decrease in symptoms over a period of six months. Sounds great, right?

Imagine, now, that this particular site gets a little Google juice. And let's say that somebody hits that site one day, not knowing that it was part of a fictional universe—worse, not even knowing that there was a fictional universe it might have been a part of.

Let's say this person happens to have Parkinson's disease. And he makes a treatment decision based on your fiction.

This is very obviously a bad outcome, both for you and for the bystander. That's not to say it's entirely your fault, as a creator; surely it's incumbent upon everyone to make informed decisions and do a little more research, and it should be plain that you can't believe everything you read (especially on the Internet). But you need to think about whom you might fool and what the cost might be.

KEEPING YOUR NOSE CLEAN

We've long accepted an ideal that says that your job as a transmedia creator is to be as authentic as possible. We wind up making bad ethical choices not on purpose, but because we are so focused on the totally immersive player experience that we never stop to think about the potential consequences.

Longtime players of transmedia games develop a keen sensitivity for fakey-fake sites, but the end result is that genuine companies can look strangely fictional to our eyes. Take Lockheed Martin, a multibillion-dollar company. To my jaded eyes, the production values on its website are so low that it triggers my automatic suspicion that it's a fake. But of course it's a real company that simply doesn't put much priority on its public-facing web presence, and why should it? It sells to the government, not to me.

We're lucky we have Snopes fighting the good fight against disinformation. But do we want our creations to wind up on Snopes? How do we do right by our players and by the innocent bystanding public at the same time? What's the right thing, anyway? What do we gain and lose with various approaches to ethical transmedia?

Sadly, I don't have a lot of hard-and-fast answers. There is too much unexplored territory in transmedia for us to bow to one-size-fits-all proclamations. But I aim to put as much information in front of creators as I can, so that the choices you make are at least informed and intentional. And in my opinion, before you launch any project, you need to ask yourself four basic questions:

1. **Can this get me sued or arrested?** Obviously you don't want to break the law or incite your players to break the law, even by mistake.

2. **What's the potential harm to somebody who thinks this might be real?** Think about this in terms of both your audience and bystanders who might encounter your content out of context.

3. **Can somebody get hurt from participating in this?** This is particularly the case for events that take place in physical spaces; a live game on the West Coast some years ago resulted in a player falling down an abandoned mine shaft during play, becoming a paraplegic, and ultimately reaching a $10 million settlement with the development team. Safety first, kids.

4. **Who else does stuff like this?** Examine your methods to make sure you're not engaging in behaviors that spammers or con artists also use, like collecting money on behalf of a fictional charity. There's a fine line between fiction and outright fraud.

That's not to say that you should never, ever spring anything on an unwitting audience. Art is a huge and magnificent undertaking, and any hard-and-fast rules that I make could undermine something wonderful.

Look at Improv Everywhere. This is a group of performers who get together to throw surprise shows in the real world, with an audience of whoever happens to be in that location that day. They've variously thrown an impromptu wedding for a couple who was just wed at City Hall, staged a musical about needing napkins to clean up a spill in a mall food court, had dozens of people freeze motionless for a full minute in Grand Central Station in New York City, and brought unabridged ESPN-style hoopla to a Little League baseball game, complete with concessions, a giant video scoreboard, and color announcers.

The idea of getting informed consent or drawing your magic circle ahead of such a performance is laughable. Their art works only because of their apparent spontaneity, because of that electric moment when the audience isn't quite sure what's going on. Asking everyone to sign a waiver ahead of time would ruin the moment. There just wouldn't be a point to it anymore.

Likewise, it's possible that whatever it is you're doing might be ruined by informing the audience ahead of time. Your rule of thumb: make sure that your surprise is designed to create delight in the audience members when they catch on, not anger or betrayal. People like surprises. But they don't like to be fooled.

Q&A: BRIAN CLARK

Brian Clark, a founder of GMD Media, has a history of working extremely close to the edge between fiction and reality. His work includes indie film and immersive experiences, TV series, and big, splashy marketing productions, as detailed in the interview.

Q: *Can you tell me a little about your favorite projects?*

A: I'm probably best known for some of the commercial projects we've done over the years, including the tongue-in-cheek immersive conspiracy thriller *Beta-7* for SEGA's *ESPN NFL Football* and the big-budget action thriller *The Art of the Heist* for Audi, but I'm probably more proud of the deep online experience for Fox Television's *FreakyLinks*, which really set the bar high on how personally immersive a television experience could be. And as amazing and rule-breaking as those kinds of commercial experiences can be, our noncommercial work is where we really get to put our mad scientist caps on, so there is a special place in my heart for our 2002 transmedia film *Nothing So Strange* and our ongoing series of techno-Lovecraftian critiques of society in the *Eldritch Errors* series.

Q: *What are the advantages to blurring the line between fact and fiction a little (or a lot!) more?*

A: Artistically, I like to believe that we have the opportunity to create a sense of wonder about the world around us, to wake people up from plodding through life with a little moment that can start to open the doors of perception and unlock a sense of power to remake the world the way you want it to be. For at least the last decade, much of my work at least incorporates elements of this ideal of "reality hacking," but you see that much more obviously on the surface in our independent work than in our client work, and probably never as deeply as we did on *Nothing So Strange*, where the entire premise revolves around a documentary looking at the enduring controversy surrounding Bill Gates's assassination in 1999 in Los Angeles.

The very premise that filmmakers would do something like that sparked controversy for almost two years before our first screening in 2002, but people who have seen the film realize that Bill Gates has very little to do with the film (beyond serving as a replacement for JFK or Martin Luther King or any of the other victims of famous politically motivated assassinations that shaped

the American twentieth century). The film was really about how police and governmental corruption sap our faith in our institutions, making "open and shut" cases leave behind enduring conspiracy theories: the fact that we could send actors to actual police corruption town hall meetings to deliver speeches that in our film look like they are all about the "Gates assassination cover-up." These are the kinds of moments that can come only from blurring the line. Sometimes a lot, like Haskell Wexler did with the film *Medium Cool*.

Q: *What ethical limitations do you think a creator should hold to, or at least be aware of?*

A: I think it is worth breaking thoughts about ethics into layers. The lowest common denominators are related to legal and liability—you have a responsibility to take steps to keep your audience safe, which means that if you start encouraging the audience to take risky actions, you'd better have thought through how you'll manage that. Then you've got a layer of consideration regarding trust— many transmedia techniques, especially those involving the real world, are built upon an implied trust between the storyteller and the participants (and breaking that trust even in little ways can have cascading effects on how the audience interprets other elements). Then you've got a layer on top of that related to misperception by the nonaudience: if you stage a kidnapping in public, you can't just think about the impact on your story participants; you have to think about how random bystanders might react (and what actions they might take from their misperceptions).

Ethics sits somewhere above that layer of liability, trust, and misperception—and sometimes the ethical choices you make as a storyteller can even justify bending some of those other rules. This is particularly true if you're leaning into any kind of controversy. In *Nothing So Strange*, it was an ethical choice to start the movie with the assassination of Bill Gates because we dealt with the misperception issue by setting the death in the past, rather than something that was happening right now . . . but a fan took part of what we made and changed it to look like Gates had just been shot right now, and accidentally impacted the Korean television news and stock market (http://news.bbc.co.uk/2/hi/business /2916135.stm), which made the Secret Service call me.

Q: *Would you do* Nothing So Strange *the same way now?*

A: In the most substantial ways, definitely. There are certainly new tools available now (like YouTube! And Facebook!) that weren't available then, and that would have changed the modalities we might have used (and the business models we could have pursued).

28
Get Excited and Make Things

During the writing of this book, I had a conversation with a colleague who was asking why there aren't any million-dollar design competitions for alternate reality games. Surely, he thought, the big companies have a vested interest in fostering new talent and funneling it into our field. Why isn't there more money floating around out there, just waiting for someone who has a great idea?

This is very much the wrong question to ask and the wrong attitude to have if you're serious about becoming a creator. To explain why, I'm going to need to be very frank about the darkest point in my career.

HARD TIMES

December 2007 was a really, really bad time for me. My run with *Perplex City* had ended unexpectedly in June when the second season, already in production, was scrapped. Afterward, I quickly found a job with a new game start-up that was contingent only on the funding coming through—and the contract with the investor had already been signed. As the weather grew colder, it became clearer and clearer that the ink on that funding deal was worthless. No money was in the offing (nor would it ever be).

So I was broke. Broke enough to do SEO writing and to scour Craigslist for any shady copywriting gig I could find. Worried about making mortgage payments. Trying to find a job, and failing. I kept going into New York City to have meetings and job interviews with interactive or digital ad agencies. I'd talk about games, narrative, and deep engagement; they'd talk about banner ads and SEO. It was as if I were from a different planet (or, as it turns out, as if I were from the future).

And as much as I was desperate to do paying work, I was equally hungry to do fulfilling work. *Perplex City* had been three years of incredible creative collaboration with an exceptional team, and it was gone, gone, gone. I was lonely and unproductive. I was terrified that my career as a creator had ground to a halt and would never move forward again. I was waiting for a break. Waiting for an offer. Waiting for someone to notice me and tell me what to do next. And waiting, and waiting, and waiting.

And then I started talking to my old friend and fellow Cloudmaker Jay Bushman. He had recently launched a Twitter adaptation of a Herman Melville story called *The Good Captain*. Every day for three months, *The Good Captain* spun out a few short sentences of the tale of a drifting spaceship and the robot mutiny that had led to the ship's dire situation.

I found myself profoundly jealous of Bushman's ability to create and promote something so interesting when it wasn't his job and he had no funding. What did he have that I didn't?

DIY

The answer, of course, was nothing at all. Nothing but the sheer drive to create, that is.

This ignited the spark in me that had been missing: the passion to just make something with whatever resources I had on hand. Since I was so dead broke, those resources amounted to my brain, my fingers to type with, the computer I already owned, and the Internet connection I was already paying for. (Even the Internet connection and the computer are negotiable; libraries across the United States and in many countries offer computers with Internet access free to the public.)

But Twitter is free. So I made Madame Zee, a Twitter account to tell horoscopes. It was just a tiny little project, a single tweet a day, and it never found a mass audience. All the same, it felt absolutely amazing to be making something new and putting it out into the world.

Some time later, I decided to experiment with Google Calendars as a vehicle for narrative, testing my theory that anything at all can tell a story if you try hard enough. I made a short time travel story called *Circular Logic* and posted it to my blog. Other small-scale personal projects followed: a collaborative wiki fiction experiment called *Voices*; a group writing challenge called *My Super First Day*.

I'll be the first to admit that none of these things were exceptional in execution or in concept. They are by far not my finest work. But that's not the point anyway; the point is that in pursuing my vision, I joined the ranks of indie filmmakers, artists, and writers who know (and have always known) that if you're passionate enough and you're willing to put in the time to develop the necessary skills, you'll find a way to be creative—even without venture capital, grants, or contracts.

A curious correlation arose. The more indie stuff I made, the more paying work I got, too, and on an amazing array of projects. Why? There are a lot of people who talk about transmedia. It turns out that there are precious few who are actually trying to make something with what they have right now. Since then, I've had the great privilege of working on a number of high-profile projects with some of the finest and most talented creators in the field.

Don't keep calm and carry on
Creative Commons Attribution Noncommercial Sharealike art by Matt Jones. Used with permission.

And it's nothing special about me; you can do it, too. Just prove that you have the ambition to create, no matter what your situation. That puts you at a decided advantage.

So my biggest, most important lesson is this: you can't wait for permission or funding or a contract or a job. Once you get this—and I mean really, really get this—you and your career will be transformed. You will be liberated. Don't hang around hoping that somebody specifically asks you to make something. Find something to get excited about, and then, as the Nike ads go, Just Do It.

There has never been a more exciting time to be a storyteller, and we're sitting on the brink of a whole new art form. We don't know what it's going to look like when it grows up, but that means that we can try just about anything we want.

Take a deep breath, and then jump into it. You won't regret it.

ADDITIONAL RESOURCES

Film and game industry publications like *Variety*, *IndieWire*, *AdAge*, and *The Escapist* sometimes cover transmedia, as do consumer publications like *Wired*, *Salon*, and *Newsweek*. But here are a select few more targeted news sources and blogs to learn from:

Transmedia Talk. This weekly podcast, hosted by Nick Braccia, Haley Moore, and Dee Cook, offers analysis of the space and interviews with some of the most fascinating creators in transmedia today. Transmedia Talk is hosted by the Workbook Project. http://workbookproject.com

StoryForward. This fascinating podcast hosted by Steve Peters and J. C. Hutchins features deep interviews about process and practice with luminaries of the transmedia scene. http://www.storyforwardpodcast.com

ARGNet. Originally a blog covering alternate reality games, this site has since branched out to cover all manner of transmedia projects. Sometimes these articles are syndicated to the Wired Decode blog, which is also worth a look. http://www.argn.com

MovieViral. Like ARGNet, this blog once focused exclusively on viral marketing campaigns for films, but has since expanded to report on a variety of transmedia projects. http://www.movieviral.com

Universe Creation 101/You Suck at Transmedia. Dr. Christy Dena's thoughts on transmedia production and the creative process. She brings the hard-won wisdom of experience to her work. http://www.yousuckattransmedia.com

Unfiction. This site features an online forum that is the heart of the hardcore ARG community, but it also discusses wider transmedia projects at great length and with great frequency. This is an excellent community to understand if you're planning any interactive elements. http://www.unfiction.com

Transmythology. Simon Pulman of Starlight Runner blogs about the business and production side of transmedia. His analysis is often very insightful. http://transmythology.com

CONFERENCES

There are a number of conferences focusing on transmedia storytelling throughout the year that you might consider attending to meet potential clients and collaborators, and to build stronger ties with the overall community of transmedia creators.

Power to the Pixel. This London-based conference springs from the indie film community. Many excellent talks from prior years are available online. http://www.powertothepixel.com

TEDx Transmedia. TEDx Transmedia may not be an annual event, but the talks from 2010 are available online. http://www.tedxtransmedia.com

StoryWorld. The first-ever StoryWorld was held in 2011, and as of this writing another is planned in 2012. It promises to become an unmissable and exclusively transmedia-focused affair. http://www.storyworldconference.com

SXSW. This annual music, film, and interactive festival in Austin isn't solely focused on transmedia, but creators of transmedia works have an increasingly large presence there. This is a great conference to attend for meeting others working in the same space. Audio and even video for many of the talks are available online. http://sxsw.com

GDC. Like SXSW, the Game Developer's Conference is not exclusively focused on transmedia, but it is a great place to find more than a few creators and potential clients. http://www.gdconf.com

Acknowledgments

To begin at the beginning, I'd like to thank Guy Gonzalez for introducing me to my stellar agent, Jason Allen Ashlock of Movable Type Management Group (and thanks to you, too, Jason!). I'd also like to thank both Niki Papadopoulos for her vote of confidence and my editor, Donya Dickerson, at McGraw-Hill, along with Casie Vogel, Pattie Amoroso, and Alice Manning, who did all the hard work to get this book polished and printed.

Thanks to my husband, Matt, and my girls, Sasha and Maya, for their patience and grace while I wrote this book—and in all the years before, when I was learning everything that went into it the hard way. A million thanks to all those in my family for their love and support: my mom and dad and siblings, step-relations and in-laws alike. I love every one of you, and don't you forget it.

Very, very special thanks to all the Q&A interviewees in this book for going above and beyond, and for teaching me so much in the first place: Naomi Alderman, Michael Andersen, Yomi Ayeni, Nina Bargiel, Caitlin Burns, Jay Bushman,

Brian Clark, Christy Dena, Adrian Hon, J. C. Hutchins, Evan Jones, Elan Lee, Mike Monello, Sean Stewart, and Sara Thacher.

Special shout-outs, too, to Michael Andersen and Lucas Johnson for keeping me honest; to Naomi Alderman, Adrian Hon, Andrew Cohen, Haley Moore, Jay Bushman, Tom Bridge, J. C. Hutchins, and Sharrow for keeping me sane; and of course to all the Cloudmakers, most especially the #evanchan crew, for making me crazy in the first place. I wouldn't be here if it weren't for you.

Index

About the Author

Andrea Phillips is an award-winning transmedia writer, game designer, and author. Her work includes a variety of educational and commercial projects, including *The Maester's Path* for HBO's *Game of Thrones* with Campfire Media, *America 2049* with human rights nonprofit Breakthrough, *Routes Game* for Channel 4 Education, and the independent commercial ARG *Perplex City*. These projects have variously won the Prix Jeunesse Interactivity Prize, a Broadband Digital award, a BIMA, an IVCA Grand Prix award, the Origins Vanguard Innovation Award, and others.

Her indie work includes the Kickstarted collaboration *Balance of Powers*, the ongoing Twitter horoscopes of Madame Zee, and the forthcoming serial transmedia project *Felicity*.

Andrea is a comoderator for the first community of ARG players, the Cloudmakers, and a Fellow of the Futures of Entertainment. She has spoken at SXSW, MIT Storytelling 3.0, the Power to the Pixel/IFP Cross-Media Forum, ARGfest, DIY Days, and FITC Storytelling X.1, among others.

Andrea cheats at solitaire (a victimless crime) and *Words with Friends* (which is less forgivable). Consider yourself warned.